W9-CPC-987

The Corrupt Classroom

Pacific Research Institute
101 Montgomery Street, Suite 1300
San Francisco, CA 94104
Tel: 415-989-0833
www.pacificresearch.org

The Corrupt Classroom:
Bias, Indoctrination, Violence and Social Engineering
Show Why America Needs School Choice

By Lance T. Izumi
with Cassidy Syftestad and Christie Syftestad

June 2017

ISBN: 978-1-934276-35-8

The Corrupt Classroom:
Bias, Indoctrination, Violence and Social Engineering Show Why America Needs School Choice

By Lance Izumi
with Cassidy Syftestad and
Christie Syftestad

The Corrupt Classroom:
Bias, Indoctrination, Violence and
Social Engineering Show Why
America Needs School Choice

by Lance Izumi
with Cassidy Syftestad and
Christie Syftestad

To Rikio and Mikuri Izumi, whose love and kindness are such a blessing to their children and grandchildren, and to all American parents who want the education that best meets the needs of their children.

Contents

Contents

Introduction

Introduction

When supporters of school choice argue that parents should be empowered to choose the best schooling option for their children's individual needs, whether that be a regular public, public charter, private or homeschool option, they almost always buttress their argument by relying on school and student performance data to show that public schools are academically failing or underperforming compared to other schooling options. Yet, there are many equally or even more important reasons for supporting school-choice options for parents and their children than academic performance.

There are many academic performance measures, often standardized test scores, showing that U.S. public school students are not performing well in the core academic subjects. The Program for International Student Assessment (PISA) is a worldwide exam administered every three years that measures mathematics, reading, and science knowledge and skills of 15-year-olds in 72 countries.

In December 2016, scores for the 2015 PISA were released, showing that the performance of U.S. students dropped significantly in math. From 2012 to 2015, the average math score for U.S. students fell by 11 points, which resulted in the U.S. ranking tumbling down from 28th to 35th. Indeed, U.S. students performed below the worldwide average in math.[1]

The average math scores also fell from 2013 to 2015 on the fourth- and eighth-grade National Assessment of Educational Progress (NAEP), often referred to as the "nation's report card." The drop, in fact, was the first time there had been a decline in mathematics proficiency on the NAEP since the math exam was first given to public school students in 1990. There was also a drop in the eighth-grade reading scores.[2]

At the state level, new exams aligned to the Common Core national education standards and curricula have shown generally low student performance in math and reading.

In California in 2016, only 48 percent, less than half, of students met grade-level standards in English, while a little more than a third, 37 percent, met the grade-level standards in mathematics.[3]

Given the poor performance of public school students on these tests, it is not surprising that much research comparing the performance of public school students with those students that use a school-choice instrument, such as a voucher, conclude that the choice students perform at a higher level than their public school peers.

Greg Forster, in his study "A Win-Win Solution: The Empirical Evidence for School Choice," written for the Friedman Foundation for Educational Choice, now renamed EdChoice, found:

> Eighteen empirical studies have examined academic outcomes for school choice participants using random assignment, the gold standard of social science. Of those, 14

find choice improves student outcomes: six find all students benefit and eight find some benefit and some are not visibly affected. Two studies find no visible effect, and two studies find Louisiana's voucher program—where most of the eligible private schools were scared away from the program by an expectation of hostile future action from regulators—had a negative effect. [4]

Forster concludes that the "few outlier studies" that do not fit the pattern of choice programs increasing student performance should not detract from the "consensus in favor of school choice as a general policy.[5] Others are not quite as sanguine.

The authors of one of the Louisiana studies point out, "One of the central debates about school reform is whether or not school choice improves student outcomes."[6] And indeed, the centrality of student outcomes to the debate over school choice could end up boxing choice proponents into a corner when research, such as the Louisiana studies, shows a decline in performance of students using choice instruments. Yet, focusing exclusively on student performance measures ignores the many other reasons why parents may want to use choice tools to send their children to another school other than the neighborhood regular public school.

Many parents, for example, are rightly concerned about the growing politicization of the classroom. Outbursts from educators during the recent presidential election are but the tip of the political-bias iceberg. Far from being mere anecdotal incidents—and there are a lot of those—political bias is becoming systemic in public school systems and has turned many public schools into indoctrination centers for progressive ideologies and causes.

Curricula are often chosen by school officials with little input from parents, who only find out about the materials when their children bring home their textbooks.

Also, parents are, for obvious reasons, concerned about the safety of their children when they go to school. If they feel that their children may be harmed because of gangs, bullying, rogue teachers, unhealthy peer culture, or lax school discipline policies, parents will want to find safer schooling options, regardless of their performance on standardized tests.

Further, if parents find that school officials ignore their concerns, then it becomes sensible for them to seek out schooling alternatives.

And if education officials mismanage resources causing negative impacts on students, then why should parents want to continue to send their children to schools run by those officials?

All of these reasons outlined in this book, plus many others, have nothing to do with academic performance of schools and students, yet are understandable reasons for parents to demand that they be empowered to choose different schooling options for their children. This book explores these non-academic-performance reasons in detail.

Chapter One: Political and Ideological Bias in the Classroom

Political and Ideological Bias in the Classroom

For years, school choice efforts have mainly focused on the poor performance of traditional public schools. Growing political bias in the classroom, however, is just as important a reason to give parents the ability to choose where and how their children receive their schooling.

While rising for some time, the 2016 presidential campaign seemed to supercharge bias in the classroom.

At the national level, Randi Weingarten, head of the American Federation of Teachers, claimed that there is a so-called "Trump Effect" that promotes "a climate of bullying" in schools.[7]

Not to be outdone, Weingarten's union counterpart at the rival National Education Association, Lily Eskelsen Garcia, also cited the "Trump Effect," stating at a pro-Hillary Clinton union press conference, "Donald Trump sets an example that teaches the wrong lesson." Garcia claimed, "The rise in vitriolic speech in classrooms and the anxiety this causes for some of our most vulnerable students shows that Trump's rhetoric is far more damaging than previously imagined."[8]

Garcia's claims are based on an unscientific survey by the left-wing Southern Poverty Law Center of its own teacher email subscribers and website visitors. Even the SPLC admitted that its survey "is not a random sample of teachers nationally," and, further, "those who chose to respond to our survey are likely to be those who are most concerned about the impact of the presidential campaign on their students and schools."[9] In other words, respondents were those who were likely to be the most politically motivated.

Yet, the "Trump Effect" campaign talking points filtered down to state and local officials who then turned the talking points into biased classroom instruction.

In San Francisco, the teachers union, the United Educators of San Francisco, issued an anti-Trump lesson plan that could be used by its 6,000 members. In a letter to school district staff by the plan's author, high school social studies teacher Fakhra Shah, Trump is labeled a "racist and sexist man" who has "become president of our country by pandering to a huge racist and sexist base."[10]

The lesson plan itself is clearly unbalanced. For example, while students are asked to create a poster that would address Trump supporters and a poster that would address Clinton supporters, students are only asked to discuss the Trump poster through the lens of, "How we will not engage in dehumanizing those who dehumanize us."[11]

The resources recommended by the lesson plan include articles, reports, and videos by leftist publications, organizations, and individuals such as *Mother Jones* magazine, the Southern Poverty Law Center and producer/director Michael Moore.[12] No mainstream resources are recommended for balance.

While the union's lesson plan includes the fig-leaf statement, "Students feel safe and respected (whether they are for or against Trump)," pro-Trump students will certainly not feel safe when the document asks the rhetorical question: "How to change the minds of so many in America who are so racist, sexist, etc."[13]

The plan exhorts teachers to tell students "we must and will fight for justice against an unjust system and an unjust people" and "we will keep fighting."[14]

How are undecided students able to choose a candidate to support if one candidate is already labeled racist, sexist, or unjust? Or in the context of the 2016 election, how is a pro-Trump student supposed to feel when he or she is characterized by teachers as racist, sexist, and unjust? And given the violence perpetrated by left-wing extremists in the wake of President Trump's election, how safe are pro-Trump students supposed to feel when teachers are calling on their students to fight against the so-called beliefs held by the pro-Trump students? There is no acknowledgement of the chilling effect on free speech in general and specifically on the ability of students to make up their own minds about the candidates.

Examples also abound of teachers across the country who engaged in politicized instruction based on their anti-Trump political bias.

Yvette Felarca is a teacher at Martin Luther King Middle School in Berkeley. She is also the leader of the radical By Any Means Necessary organization, which the *San Jose Mercury News* described "as a 'militant' group that uses a variety of tactics, including violence, to spread its message."[15]

According to the *Daily Californian*, Felarca was part of an April 2017 anti-free-speech counter-protest that stated, on its Facebook page, its goal of shutting down a Berkeley free speech rally before it began.

"We're here to take a stand," Felarca said, "against the whole Trump administration."[16] Felarca was also a leader in a previous protest in February 2017 at UC Berkeley that devolved into violence.

As CNN reported at the time, "The violent protesters tore down metal barriers, set fires near the campus bookstore and damaged the construction site of a new dorm."[17] Many people were injured by this rampaging mob.

In June 2016, Felarca reportedly shoved a man to the ground at a demonstration in Sacramento. The brawl resulted in seven people being stabbed. Felarca told the *Mercury News,* that the First Amendment should not protect speech with which she disagrees and that she labels "hate speech."[18]

Even parents in ultraliberal Berkeley were appalled by Felarca's actions. Many took to social media to complain that, according to the *Mercury News,* "her violent, in-your-face message has no place in the classroom, especially at a school named after an activist who preached for social change through nonviolence."

"A person like that should not be an educator," said Cindy Berck, a mother of a Berkeley student. "It crosses the line in terms of modeling behavior."[19]

In May 2017, a Colorado high school teacher put a photo of President Trump on a piñata for students to hit. Students took photos of the activity, which then eventually went viral on social media.

"It is disturbing that this would be happening in a school setting," said parent Lesley Hollywood. "Why divide people? Why do this? There are so many other ways we can address politics in schools."[20]

In Staten Island, New York, officials at Paulo Intermediate School reprimanded a sixth-grade English teacher for a vocabulary homework assignment that disparaged President Trump. Students had to complete fill-in-the-blank sentences, choosing from a list of words provided by the teacher. The anti-Trump sentence read:

President Trump speaks in a very superior
and _____ manner insulting many
people. He needs to be more _____
so that the American people respect and
admire him.[21]

The correct words to fill in the blanks were "haughty" and "humble."

Vincent Ungro, whose 11-year-old daughter came home with the assignment and who is a strong supporter of President Trump, had his daughter turn in the assignment without filling in the blanks. In addition, he wrote on the bottom of the sheet, "Please keep your political views to yourself and do not try to influence my daughter." The teacher, however, marked down Ungro's daughter for failing to fill in the blanks and then claimed that she was not expressing a political view. Ungro alerted school officials, who then issued the letter of reprimand to the teacher for exercising "poor judgment."[22]

Ungro said that the teacher should have avoided political references:

First, I don't think that putting your personal feelings about politics into a sixth-grader's homework is proper. There were at least a thousand sentences that she could have used besides disparaging our president.[23]

In Mountain View, California, a history teacher was suspended after he lectured students on the parallels between the rise of Trump and Adolf Hitler. Both Trump and Hitler, said the teacher, wanted to "make their countries great again."[24]

In North Carolina, an English teacher made students compare speeches by Trump and Hitler.[25]

Such open attacks on Donald Trump and his supporters caused great discomfort to many students. One father who complained said:

> My son was very uncomfortable. He felt like she was attacking anybody who liked Trump or anybody's parents who liked Trump. She didn't say anything bad about any other politician.[26]

According to the United Kingdom's *Daily Mail*, parents did not want to reveal their identities to the news media because they were concerned that the "very liberal" school administration would exact retribution. One father told Fox News columnist Todd Starnes about the fear and helplessness felt by parents:

> Most conservative parents don't want to fight the system because they know they are going to be shouted down. Every parent is reticent to speak out because we are afraid the school board will come after us. We've seen them do that in the past.[27]

In Dallas, Texas, a high school art teacher showed a photograph of Donald Trump on her classroom projector screen, then whipped out a water gun, squirted the image and yelled, "Die!" A video was taken of the teacher pretending to assassinate the president, and the teacher subsequently uploaded it to her Instagram account on Inauguration Day. The video went viral, catching the attention of the school district officials and the Secret Service. The teacher was suspended by the school district.[28]

In Portsmouth, New Hampshire, a high school math teacher dressed up as Donald Trump and then danced to a rap song that included profane language. Michael Grondahl, whose son was a student in the class, said that his son texted him to tell him that the teacher "was making fun" of Trump in the classroom. According to Grondahl:

> He texted us and he felt very uncomfortable. It's not even like this was a sociology teacher. This is a geometry teacher.[29]

In Houston, Texas, a high school student said that his teacher offered extra credit to students for attending an anti-Trump demonstration during the presidential campaign. At a press conference, the student said, "I didn't go, so I didn't get extra credit. I don't know if anybody got it, but that's what she proposed for extra credit."[30] The teacher used her grading power to promote her political beliefs on to students.

It is important to point out, however, that political and ideological bias in the classroom is not limited to discussions of the recent presidential campaign.

In Norman, Oklahoma, a high school philosophy teacher lectured students by stating, "to be white is to be racist, period."[31] A stunned biracial student recorded the teacher's remarks and later told a local news station:

> Half of my family is Hispanic, so I just felt like, you know, him calling me racist just because I'm white . . . I mean, where's your proof in that . . . I felt like he was encouraging people to kind of pick on people for being white.[32]

The father of the student observed, "Why is it okay to demonize one race to children that you are supposed to be teaching a curriculum to?"[33]

In Des Moines, Iowa, an activist with the radical leftist Occupy Wall Street movement was invited to speak to students at a local middle school. The father of one student found out about the invitation and sat in on the activist's presentation.

"I was amazed they would allow someone like that to come in and talk to the students," he told a Fox News interviewer. "He came in and said how evil the military is and how he used to respect the police and how he doesn't respect the police anymore."[34]

According to Fox News, the father said no one was there to refute or argue against the Occupier's allegations: "I told the principal I thought it was pretty egregious that they would bring someone like that in but the principal didn't think there was anything wrong with it."[35]

School officials in these cases seem to think nothing about inviting those who encourage racial tension in the classroom.

Meantime, conservatives often have the welcome mat pulled out from under them by school officials.

In Montana, Marine Corps veteran Gerald Molen, who won an Academy Award for co-producing the acclaimed movie "Schindler's List," was scheduled to speak to seniors at Ronan High School, but 90 minutes before his speech he was told by the school's principal that he could not speak because he was "too right wing." Despite the fact that his talk was going to be apolitical, the principal never bothered to even ask about the content of his speech:

> He was concerned about my presentation.
> No, he didn't ask me of the content. No,
> he didn't ask to read the speech for any
> clarification as to content. No, he would
> not tell me who the complaining party or
> parties were, nor would he give me any

further explanation. Just that there would be no presentation by me that day.[36]

Molen went to say:

For the record, my presentation that day had nothing political or capricious that would be harmful to a senior high school student (or even a grammar school student) or a teacher. It dealt with my hopes for their futures. It was a cheerleading presentation that allowed me to remind them of their individual greatness and opportunities for the future. My intent was to inspire and motivate those looking for an encouraging word and message of hope beyond the walls of the institution they were leaving to the next chapter in their young lives. It spoke to the contributions and greatness of their teachers, administrators, parents, and peers but with an emphasis on their ability to conceive, to believe, and to achieve. But I guess I was wrong about teachers and/or school administrators.[37]

Molen asked rhetorically, "In America today, are children taught or indoctrinated?" He answers his own question saying that students "were indoctrinated with a sense of fear and mistrust that a fellow Montanan just might stand before them and say something some official school administrator deemed 'possibly harmful.'"[38]

Ideological bias is not limited to individual classrooms, schools or school districts. It is also a systemic problem due to the often one-sidedness of state curriculum guidelines. California is a good example.

The Golden State's history and social studies curriculum framework, which serves a guide for the state's public schools and teachers, is weighted overwhelmingly toward a liberal viewpoint on interpreting history.

Take, for example, the treatment of communism and the Cold War. In describing the Cold War, the curriculum framework says:

> It was soon clear that there would be an ideological and geopolitical struggle with consequences rippling across the globe between the Soviet Union, a Communist nation with an authoritarian government that had a very poor record of protecting human rights . . . and a vision of foreign policy bent on creating and supporting Communist Nations and the United States, a capitalist-leaning nation with an elected government and a vision of foreign policy bent on supporting other capitalist-leaning nations.[39]

The Soviet Union was not just a regime with "a very poor record of protecting human rights," as the curriculum framework euphemistically describes. Through politically motivated forced starvations, mass executions, and other heinous means, the Soviet Union was responsible for the deaths of 20 million people.[40] The Soviet Union did not just fail to protect human rights. Rather, it was a killing machine of gargantuan proportions.

Given that the United States faced such an adversary, the framework is wrong to effectively reduce the Cold War to a moral equivalent of the Soviet Union supporting "other Communist Nations" and the United States "supporting other capitalist-leaning nations." The late

Jeanne Kirkpatrick, U.S. ambassador to the United Nations under President Ronald Reagan and one of the intellectual architects of the Reagan administration's foreign policy, condemned the moral-equivalence characterization of the Cold War conflict between the Soviet Union and the United States. Such a characterization fails to understand the nature of communist ideology, which is a universalist philosophy that seeks to impose its tenets on all mankind.

The intellectual dishonesty of California's curriculum framework is nowhere better displayed than in the description of Mao Zedong, the founder and longtime ruler of communist China:

> After a long civil war, communists led by Mao Zedong, came to power in China, expanding the geographic scope of the Cold War. . . . The Great Leap Forward (1958-1961) and the Cultural Revolution (1966-1976) caused massive turmoil in China. Students should learn about the unrest and disorder in China during these years: elites were made to work on farms; there was arbitrary application of revolutionary justice; the Red Guard even turned on members of Mao's own party.[41]

Terms such as "massive turmoil," "unrest," and "disorder" are euphemisms of appalling dimensions when used to describe The Great Leap Forward and the Cultural Revolution.

According to *The Black Book of Communism*, published by Harvard University and which is generally regarded as the most authoritative work on the legacy of communism, 20 million to 43 million ordinary Chinese died in the massive famine caused by the forced communist agricultural policies imposed by the Mao regime in The Great Leap Forward, which made it the worst famine in the history of the world. [42]

Amongst the unbelievable atrocities committed during The Great Leap Forward, *The Black Book* notes that children were killed, boiled, and used for fertilizer, while in various provinces children were eaten. According to one young communist idealist whose eyes were opened by talking to peasants years after The Great Leap Forward:

> Before my eyes, among the weeds, rose up one of the scenes I had been told about, one of the banquets at which the families had swapped children in order to eat them. I could see the worried faces of the families as they chewed the flesh of other people's children. . . . What had made them swallow that human flesh, amidst the tears and grief of other parents – flesh that they would never have imagined tasting, even in their worst nightmares?[43]

The young communist idealist then had his epiphany as to who and what was to blame for this mind-boggling tragedy:

> In that moment I understood what a butcher he had been, the man "whose like humanity has not seen in several centuries, and China not in several thousand years": Mao Zedong. Mao Zedong and his henchmen, with their criminal political system, had driven parents mad with hunger and led them to hand over their own children over to others, and to receive the flesh of

others to appease their own hunger. Mao Zedong, to wash away the crime that he had committed in assassinating democracy, had launched the Great Leap Forward, and obliged thousands and thousands of peasants dazed by hunger to kill one another with hoes, and to save their own lives thanks to the flesh and blood of their childhood companions. They were not the real killers; the real killers were Mao Zedong and his companions.[44]

In other provinces, "the stated intention was to keep the red flag flying even if 99 percent of the population died," so communist cadres "returned to the traditional practices of live burials and torture with red-hot irons."[45]

The enormity of these crimes against humanity is so much more egregious than the curriculum framework's milquetoast example of "elites were made to work on farms" that one cannot help but conclude that pure ideological bias is at work.

In addition, no mention is made in the curriculum framework of the fact that one to three million Chinese were killed during Mao's Cultural Revolution.[46]

All told, *The Black Book* estimates that 65 million people were killed by communism in China.[47]

The death toll of communism worldwide during the 20th Century is estimated to be between 85 million to 100 million.[48] The curriculum framework fails to mention that crucial basic fact when discussing communism and the Cold War. Without a full understanding of the inherent immorality of communism, students can never understand the real nature of the basis for the Cold War.

The failure of the curriculum regarding the true nature of communism naturally has an impact on one of the most important events in American history of the second half of the 20th Century – the Vietnam War.

As in the general discussion of the Cold War and communism, the curriculum framework fails to give a balanced perspective on crucial aspects of the Vietnam War. For example, one of the darkest chapters in America's involvement in Vietnam was the My Lai Massacre of 1968 where up to 500 Vietnamese civilians, including children, were massacred by U.S. troops. The curriculum framework says:

> Recording in the haze of war, American journalists reported on television what urban warfare and guerrilla fighting entailed; in this context Americans started to call into question the principles upon which the war was being fought. By the time of the Tet Offensive and the My Lai Massacre in early 1968, American public opinion had turned against the war effort.[49]

Yet, the framework fails to mention that in the aftermath of the Tet Offensive, the Vietnamese communists massacred 3,000 people, including Vietnamese Catholic priests, French religious workers, German doctors, plus government officials and workers.[50]

Indeed, the framework says nothing about the aftermath of the Vietnam War, where up to one million Vietnamese were sent to communist re-education camps.[51] All told, Vietnamese communism in the 20th Century was responsible for the deaths of one million people.[52] Without this factual information, it is impossible for students to develop a full understanding of the war, why it was fought, and what was truly lost when the United States pulled out of Vietnam and the country fell to the communists.

The curriculum framework is also skewed to the left when it comes to subject matter to be studied.

It highlights the leaders, issues, positions, legislative and court successes, and varied membership of the feminist movement. While the section says that students can read works by opponents of feminism, those opponents, their arguments and philosophies, and their affiliations are not specifically mentioned or included. For example, Phyllis Schlafly, the conservative constitutional lawyer, author and political activist, who led the successful campaign to defeat the Equal Rights Amendment (ERA) is not mentioned at all. This is despite the fact that experts such as political scientist Jane Mansbridge concluded:

> Many people who followed the struggle over the ERA believed—rightly in my view—that the Amendment would have been ratified by 1975 or 1976 had it not been for Phyllis Schlafly's early and effective effort to organize potential opponents.[53]

As historian Judith Glazer-Raymo noted, ERA supporters failed "to take seriously the power of the family values argument and the single-mindedness of Schlafly and her followers." In Glazer-Raymo's judgment, "The ERA's defeat seriously damaged the women's movement, destroying its momentum and its potential to foment social change."[54] Yet, this broader and more complete perspective on the feminist movement is missing from California's curriculum framework.

Further, the modern conservative movement, which succeeded in electing Californian Ronald Reagan as president, with its complex mixture of social, economic, and national security sub-movements, is given comparatively brief mention, with no key figures cited or references provided.

As a state document, the curriculum framework ensures that this bias will be systemic throughout California public schools.

The bottom line is that politicizing the classroom negatively affects students. As *The Economist* points out, "Students who dissent from the teacher's view may feel alienated from the discussion and uncomfortable expressing their ideas openly."

Further, "Younger, more impressionable children with [undeveloped] understanding of politics may be confused if they hear their parents supporting candidate X while their teacher insists on candidate Y."

The magazine concludes, "Either way, it seems a mistake to make political advocacy a main thrust of the school day."[55] However, if some schools insist on politicizing instruction, then children should be able to escape such indoctrination through school choice tools such as intra and inter-district transfer programs, charter schools, and private-school choice programs such as education savings accounts.

Chapter Two: Unsafe Environments

Unsafe Environments

Perhaps no other issue will cause a parent to want to take their child out of a school than when the child's safety is in question. School-related crime and other disruptive activities are a tremendous concern for parents. There have been many instances of appalling crimes on school campuses, ranging from peer-to-peer bullying to classroom sexual assaults that make every parent shudder with fear for the safety of their own children.

Student-on-Student Crime

In February 2017, a 9-year-old Alabama girl, Lanny Turpin, was brutally attacked at her elementary school in the town of Sheffield. She and some classmates were walking to an art class when another student grabbed her.

Lanny's attacker jumped on top of her, causing her to hit her head on a pole before falling to the pavement. Among her injuries, she sustained a concussion, two black eyes and a bruised face.

Immediately after the attack, school officials contacted Lanny's mother, Kelly Turpin, and told her that Lanny had fallen accidently and needed to be picked up.

Upon arriving at the school, Kelly Turpin was shocked to find her daughter covered in blood. The school nurse told her that Lanny had fallen down and started to tell Kelly about the incident. However, Lanny interrupted and said that the incident was not an accident and that she had been attacked: "No Momma, I told them she grabbed me and jumped on top of me."[56] She said that her attacker had not wanted her to be friends with anyone else, and reacted when Lanny was being nice to a mentally challenged child.

Kelly Turpin was outraged, not only by the attack against her daughter, but by the response of the school:

> I want them to start stepping up to the plate with these kids. My child should be able to go to school and have an education and know they can go tell teachers or the principal what's going on.[57]

"Other mothers are in the same situation," said Kelly. Further:

> And we went through this before with my older child. Nothing has changed when we've gone to the school about the bullying. I just want them safe at school.[58]

Lanny's mother told *AL*. com, that her biggest concern is the safety of students. "When I asked the principal what was being done about the bully, he said she would be suspended for two days." However, she said, "Then I found out they didn't even do anything to her."[59] Because she feels that the school system is not doing enough to prevent and punish bullying, Kelly told an interviewer that she is going to start homeschooling her daughter.[60]

What happened in Alabama, however, is not an isolated incident. National statistics show that crime in the country's public schools is widespread, and the impact on victims is often devastating.

The U.S. Department of Education and the U.S. Department of Justice released a joint annual report entitled "Indicators of School Crime and Safety" (hereinafter referred to as the "Indicators" report). At the time of the writing of this book, the latest available report was from May 2016. In that report, the authors observe: "For both students and teachers, victimization at school can have lasting effects. In addition to experiencing loneliness, depression, and adjustment difficulties, victimized children are more prone to truancy, poor academic performance, dropping out of school and violent behavior."[61] Given these impacts, the latest statistics indicate that millions of American students are suffering.

During the 2013-14 school year, an amazing 65 percent of public schools reported that one or more incidents of violence had taken place, which translated into an estimated 757,000 crimes. Certain types of schools were prone to higher rates of violent crime incidents.

Eighty-six percent of public schools with 1,000 or more students enrolled reported violent incidents at school, which was higher than the percentages reported by schools with fewer students. [62]

Public middle schools were also most likely to report violent incidents. Almost nine out of 10 middle schools, 88 percent, reported violent incidents. In contrast, 78 percent of high schools/combined elementary-secondary schools and 53 percent of elementary schools reported violent incidents.[63] These violent incidents can be broken down into specific categories of behavior.

About 58 percent of public schools reported one or more incidents of a physical attack or fight with a weapon, which translates into 453,000 incidents.[64]

Thirteen percent of public schools recorded one or more serious violent offenses, which could include threat of physical attack with a weapon, robbery without a weapon, physical attack or fight with a weapon, sexual battery other than rape, rape or attempted rape.[65]

Besides violent offenses, illegal drug use is prevalent in schools. Twenty-two percent of students in grades 9-12 reported that in 2013 illegal drugs were made available to them on school property, and 23 percent said they had used marijuana at least one time in the previous 30 days.[66]

The "Indicators" report also gives results on the School Survey on Crime and Safety (SSOCS). In the SSOCS, public school principals were asked to provide the number of thefts of $10 or more, plus other incidents that had taken place at their school. Eighty-five percent of the principals said during the 2009-10 school year, the last year where survey results are available, that such incidents had taken place at their public school.[67]

Interestingly, the SSOCS results showed that "a greater percentage of public schools recorded a criminal incident than reported a criminal incident to the police." In fact, the disparity between criminal incidents at school and those reported to police was stark:

> This pattern held true for violent incidents, serious violent incidents, thefts, and other criminal incidents. Seventy-four percent of schools recorded one or more violent incidents, 16 percent recorded one or more serious violent incidents, 44 percent recorded one or more thefts, and 68 percent recorded one or more other criminal

incidents. In comparison, 40 percent of public schools reported at least one violent incident to police, 10 percent reported at least one serious violent incident to police, 25 percent reported at least one theft to police, and 46 percent reported one or more other criminal incidents to police.[68]

The fact that more than a third of violent criminal incidents went unreported to police should surely concern parents whose children are mostly the victims of these crimes.

In St. Paul, Minnesota, in an ideologically motivated effort to promote racial equity by reducing the so-called "school-to-prison" pipeline, superintendent Valeria Silva engineered the district's adoption of a protocol that limited the interactions between the city's public schools and the police.

In her exhaustive 2017 *City Journal* article on St. Paul's disastrous school racial equity policies, Katherine Kersten, senior fellow at the Center for the American Experiment (CAE), pointed out that the district's protocol ranked five different levels of offenses. School officials were instructed to report to the police only the worst offenses, such as arson, aggravated assault and firearm possession. Other serious offenses, such as assault, sexual violence, and drug possession, were to be handled by school officials and not be reported to the police.[69] The result was a dramatic reduction in the number of crimes reported to law enforcement and prosecutors.

In 2006, school officials made 875 referrals to the local county attorney's office for various misdemeanor and felony crimes. However, by 2011, the number had dropped precipitously to only 538.[70] The reduction in referrals, however, did not indicate an improvement in student behavior, but, rather, the ideological willful blindness of top school district officials more interested in good numbers and ideological dogma. In schools and classrooms, lawlessness, chaos, and anarchy reigned.

In 2015, a veteran teacher lamented, "We have a segment of kids who consider themselves untouchable." Students invaded classrooms to assault other students. Students came to school, but did not attend class, and, instead, ran in packs through the hallways causing disruption. Riots and mass brawls became commonplace at district high schools.

A St. Paul police spokesman said, "We are witnessing more violence and serious violence." Specifically, "Fights at schools that might have been between two individuals are growing into fights between several individuals or even melees involving up to 50 people." Police were forced to use chemical sprays to break up the riots.[71]

For example, in October 2015, a mass brawl of up to 40 students broke out at one St. Paul high school. As police tried to break up the riot, school staff had forced doors closed in order to prevent many more students from joining the fracas.[72]

Katherine Kersten reported that "some high schools increasingly came to resemble war zones" and teachers "suffered injuries while resisting classroom invasions or intervening in fights."[73] Yet, according to Kersten, many of the crimes went unreported due to district policy.

One mother of a seventh-grader said that her son was viciously kicked in the groin, but "when I asked the principal why she had not contacted police, she told me, 'That's your job.'"[74]

Another mother reported that her son had been cut with a knife at school, but when she asked why the police had not been informed, she said that a school administrator drew a map to the closest police station on the back of business card and handed it to her. The mother then contacted the police who arrested one assailant for misdemeanor assault and the second assailant for a felony.[75]

Kersten noted that in a social media post, one veteran teacher said the number of "parents ignored" as "too many to count."[76]

John Choi, the local county attorney, condemned the increasing school violence as "a public health crisis."[77] Yet, all the while, the school district, ideologically wedded to its racial-equity dogma, ignored the crisis and sought scapegoats.

Social studies teacher Roy Magnuson observed, "There is an intense digging in of heels to say there is no mistake." The district pointed the finger at "people like me that have issues with racial equity and that is the reason we are challenging them." "That makes for a very convenient way of barring the reality of the situation."[78]

The bottom line is that there was a safety crisis in the St. Paul public schools, caused by the district's policies, but that crisis did not show up in the cold raw numbers of crimes reported to police. Those numbers were a fantasy, while in reality, students and teachers were assaulted on a daily basis.

It is true that some national school-crime trends have been going downward over the years. For example, the "Indicators" report says, "About 7 percent of students in grades 9-12 reported being threatened or injured with a weapon such as a gun, knife, or club on school property in 2013." The report notes, "The percentage of students who reported being threatened or injured with a weapon on school property has decreased over the last decade, from 9 percent in 2003 to 7 percent in 2013."[79] However, it is important to keep a couple of things in mind when looking at such reported trends.

First of all, there is every reason to believe that more recent data will show an increase in school crimes as a result of the Obama administration's 2014 directives to public schools to cut down on the number of suspensions and expulsions (which will be discussed shortly).

Also, any reduction in the aggregate percentage of school crimes is little comfort to a parent whose child is a victim of a specific crime. As the "Indicators" report acknowledges:

> Our nation's schools should be safe havens for teaching and learning, free of crime and violence. Any instance of crime or violence at school not only affects the individuals involved, but also may disrupt the educational process and affect bystanders, the school itself, and the surrounding community.[80]

Just among students ages 12 to 18 in 2014, there were around 850,100 non-fatal victimizations at school, which included 363,700 theft victimizations and 486,400 violent victimizations, from simple assault to serious violent victimization.[81] One can therefore imagine the negative ripple effect that reverberates through families, relatives and friends, and neighborhoods.

In fact, in 2013, 5 percent of both the nation's African-American and Hispanic students said they were afraid of being attacked or harmed at school, while 3 percent of white students reported that fear.[82] Also, 5 percent of students reported they avoided at least one activity or class or one or more places at school during the previous school year because they feared being attacked or harmed. The "Indicators" report notes, "a higher percentage of public school students (4 percent) than of private school students (1 percent) reported avoiding one or more places in school."[83]

Of course, there are non-criminal activities and behaviors that border on crime, and which can also negatively impact students. In 2013, 12 percent of students aged 12 to 18 reported that gangs were present in their school. Even more, 18 percent, of urban students reported a gang presence. Interestingly, 13 percent of public-school students, versus only 2 percent of private-school students, reported gangs in their school.[84]

Bullying is a huge concern for parents. The "Indicators" report says that 22 percent of students aged 12 to 18 were bullied at school during 2013. A significant proportion of these bullying incidents were repeat incidents. A third of students who reported being bullied at school indicated that they were bullied at least once or twice a month during the school year.[85]

Discipline and Safety-Response Measures

With so many crimes and other negative acts being committed at public schools, how are government policymakers and school administrators responding? As noted in the previous section, when a crime is committed, school officials sometimes call the police and other times they do not. Short of calling the police or expelling a student, the most common response for significant student misbehavior is suspension from school.

In 2011-12, the "Indicators" report says that 6.6 million school suspensions were handed out to students.[86] By 2013-14, the number had been reduced by 20 percent.[87] Why the precipitous drop? The steep downward trend in suspensions is due not to better student behavior, but to federal, state, and local policies that disfavored suspensions.

Opponents of suspending students for misbehavior

argue that suspensions are disproportionately imposed on African-American students and that tough disciplinary actions promote a "school-to-prison pipeline," where students who are suspended end up falling behind in school, dropping out, and being incarcerated as adults. Anti-suspension advocates have pushed for so-called "restorative justice" alternatives, which are practices aimed at changing student behavior through inclusive dialogue.[88]

Despite the lack of rigorous research showing that restorative justice is effective in changing student behavior for the better, 27 states have enacted laws that have limited the use of suspensions and other so-called "exclusionary discipline policies." A 2017 study on school discipline by the New York-based Manhattan Institute notes:

> The most sweeping . . . was California's law that imposed stricter limits on the use of suspensions for nonviolent "willful defiance" offenses. Illinois passed a law that prohibited districts from using "zero-tolerance" discipline policies and encouraged them to exhaust other options before issuing a suspension. In Georgia, students have a right to a disciplinary hearing before being suspended . . . . [89]

In addition, the Manhattan Institute study found that 53 of America's largest school districts, covering more than 6.3 million students, have revised their discipline codes to reduce the use of suspensions.[90]

At the extreme, the Los Angeles Unified School District has virtually banned suspensions, with the rate falling to near zero percent.[91]

At the federal level, just as the Obama administration pushed states to adopt the Common Core national education standards and tests, so, too, did it push states and districts to reduce the use of suspensions.

In 2014, the Obama administration's Office of Civil Rights (OCR) at the U.S. Department of Education and the Civil Rights Division of the U.S. Department of Justice issued a so-called "Dear Colleague" letter that warned school districts:

> Schools also violate Federal law when they evenhandedly implement facially neutral policies and practices that, although not adopted with the intent to discriminate, nonetheless have an unjustified effect of discriminating against students on the basis of race. The resulting discriminatory effect is commonly referred to as "disparate impact."[92]

Discipline policies that can raise disparate impact concerns, according to the government enforcers, could include "mandatory suspension, expulsion, or citation."[93]

In the wake of the Obama administration's warning, the OCR opened civil rights investigations into a number of school districts, including the Oakland Unified School District and the Oklahoma City Public Schools. Both districts agreed to reduce greatly their use of suspensions.[94]

There are major problems, however, with the anti-suspension crusade.

First of all, using disparate impact as a gauge for racial discrimination turns out to be empirically wrong. A landmark 2014 study by criminology and economics professors from the University of Cincinnati, Florida State University and the University of Texas at Dallas, which was published in the *Journal of Criminal Justice*, examined the problem behavior of suspended students prior to their suspensions.

Using long-term data from the Early Childhood Longitudinal Study, which covered a massive 21,000 children, the researchers examined "whether measures of prior problem behavior could account for the differences in suspension between both whites and blacks." Their findings were eye-opening:

> The results of these analyses were straightforward: The inclusion of a measure of prior problem behavior reduced to statistical insignificance the odds differentials in suspensions between black and white youth. Thus, our results indicate that odds differentials in suspensions are likely produced by pre-existing behavioral problems of youth that are imported into the classroom, that cause classroom disruptions, and that trigger disciplinary measures by teachers and school officials. Differences in rates of suspension between racial groups thus appear to be a function of differences in problem behaviors that emerge early in life, that remain relatively stable over time, and that materialize in the classroom.[95]

Thus, the racial disparity in suspension rates between African-American and white students can be explained by the prior problem behavior of the students, and is not the result of racism and cultural biases harbored by teachers and school officials. "Our results suggest," the researchers conclude, "that the association between school suspensions and blacks and whites reflects long-standing behavioral differences between youth and that, at least in the aggregate, the use of suspensions may not be as racially biased as many have argued."[96]

The study's authors admonished "numerous authors, interest groups, and government agencies including the Department of Justice," which "have used the racial differential in suspension rates as *prima facie* evidence of teacher or school district bias against black youth." They observed that "great liberties have been taken in linking racial differences in suspensions to racial discrimination" and, "Nowhere is this more evident than in the rhetoric surrounding the 'school-to-prison pipeline.'"[97]

The researchers caution "against the clear motivations of some scholars and activists to frame race differences in school suspensions as only a matter of discrimination or cultural bias, and especially when framed as a civil rights issue with all the corresponding threats of litigation by the federal government."[98]

"Under these circumstances," they warn, "where careers are advanced, where reputations are earned and where the 'working ideology' of scholars is confirmed, the usual critical and cautionary sway of scholarly investigation, critique, and insight becomes marginalized or usurped."[99]

Second, claims from anti-suspension advocates that suspensions cause huge lifetime costs to suspended students are highly questionable. Indeed, the Manhattan Institute study notes, "there is no rigorous causal analysis proving that suspensions have a negative effect on the student suspended."[100]

Further, and most important for parents, there is evidence that disruptive students left in the classroom have a negative impact on the learning of their fellow students. According to a study by researchers at the University of California at Davis and the University of Pittsburgh:

> Our results indicate that troubled students have a statistically significant negative effect on their peers' reading and math test

scores. Adding one troubled student to a
classroom of 20 students results in a decrease
in student reading and math test scores of
more than two-thirds of a percentile point
(2 to 3 percent of a standard deviation).[101]

In addition, a single disruptive student "also
significantly increases misbehavior of other students in
the classroom," causing them to commit 16 percent more
infractions than they otherwise would. The researchers also
found that disruptive student behavior had an especially
negative impact on higher-income children's math and
reading achievement, and on the misbehavior of low-
income children.[102]

Perhaps the most cautionary finding that the
researchers discovered was the impact of disruptive behavior
by boys on other boys:

> Across all outcome variables, both
> academic and behavioral, the negative peer
> effects appear to be driven primarily by the
> troubled boys, and these effects are largest
> on other boys in the classroom. The results
> indicate that adding one troubled boy to a
> classroom of 20 students decreases boys'
> test scores by nearly 2 percentile points
> (7 percent of a standard deviation) and
> increases the probability that a boy will
> commit a disciplinary infraction by 4.4
> percentile points (17 percent). Apparently,
> troubled boys generate the strongest
> adverse peer effects, and other boys are
> most sensitive to their influence.[103]

The researchers conclude that their findings "provide strong evidence of the validity of the 'bad apple' peer effects model, which hypothesizes that a single disruptive student can negatively affect the outcomes for all other students in the classroom."[104] If a disruptive student can have such a negative impact on his or her classmates, then the question is whether anti-suspension policies increase the level of classroom disruption, and, therefore, negatively impact non-disruptive students.

There is widespread anecdotal evidence of the recent rise in classroom disruptions as a result of anti-suspension policies. The Manhattan Institute study cites an example in Oklahoma City:

> After Oklahoma City Public Schools revised its discipline policies in response to federal pressure, one teacher told the *Oklahoman* that "[w]e were told that referrals would not require suspension unless there was blood." Another teacher in Oklahoma City reported: "Students are yelling, cursing, hitting, and screaming at teachers and nothing is being done but teachers are being told to teach and ignore behaviors . . . These students know there is nothing a teacher can do. Good students are now suffering because of the abuse and issues plaguing these classrooms."[105]

In a survey, 60 percent of Oklahoma City teachers said that the amount and frequency of offending behavior increased after the discipline reforms.[106]

Unchecked misbehavior has become a burgeoning national epidemic with terrible consequences:

In Buffalo, a teacher who got kicked in the head by a student said: "We have fights here almost every day . . . . The kids walk around and say, "We can't get suspended – we don't care what you say." One teacher told the *Fresno Bee* that "[a] student can (curse at you) and we're told that's just his personality," while another teacher reported that when she called a school resource officer about a theft, she heard one student say to the suspected thief, "Don't worry, they won't do anything." Testifying in front of the U.S. Commission on Civil Rights, a former Philadelphia teacher related that a student told him, "I'm going to torture you. I'm doing this because I can't be removed." In St. Paul, Minnesota, Ramsey County attorney noted that the number of assaults against teachers doubled from 2014 to 2015 and called the situation a "public health crisis."[107]

After discipline "reforms" had been implemented in various cities, teacher surveys found: 60 percent of Baton Rouge teachers said that they experienced an increase in violence or threats from students; 65 percent of Santa Ana, California teachers said that the new system was not working at their school; 66 percent of Syracuse teachers said that they worried about their safety at work; 67 percent of Jackson, Mississippi teachers felt their work environment felt out of control on a daily or weekly basis because of discipline issues; and 75 percent of Denver teachers disagreed that the new discipline system improved student behavior.[108]

In addition, a University of Chicago study found that Chicago Public Schools' policies making it more difficult to suspend students resulted in a negative effect on school climate. According to the study's findings, both "student and teacher reports of school climate worsened after implementation of the policy." And while anti-suspension advocates believe that fewer suspensions will result in better student outcomes, the Chicago policy did not lead to higher test scores.[109]

In St. Paul, Minnesota in 2015, veteran teacher Aaron Benner told *EAGnews,* an investigative education publication, that violent, unruly behavior in the city school district is at an all-time high, to the point where it is difficult for teachers to instruct or children to learn.[110]

As mentioned in a previous chapter, Benner, who is African American, said that African-American students in his district are frequently not held accountable for their actions. He traced this problem back to the school district's contract with the Pacific Education Group (PEG), a leftist San Francisco-based organization, that promotes the theory that "white privilege" is the cause of academic underachievement and misbehavior among African-American students. The organization recommends stopping suspensions and expulsions for bad behavior.[111]

After implementing "white privilege" training, then-superintendent Valeria Silva greatly loosened the district's discipline policies by lowering behavior expectations and dropping meaningful consequences for student misbehavior. These changes were designed to cut down on the discipline referrals of African-American students.[112]

The *Pioneer Press* (St. Paul) reported that based on PEG's advice, educators were told that they "can only chip away at achievement disparities if they confront their own racial biases and the ways racism permeates schools."[113]

"We are asking our staff to change rather than expect kids to change to fit our comfort level – and that's huge," said Stacey Kadrmas, a principal at a St. Paul-area elementary school. Yet, the *Pioneer Press* notes that, according to critics, PEG's work has alienated some educators and, "in recasting certain discipline issues as cultural misunderstandings, let disruptive students and their families off the hook." Further, despite the goal of improving student performance, there is "scarcity of solid evidence [PEG] boosts achievement."[114]

The *Pioneer Press* noted that PEG founder Glenn Singleton "balked at offering examples of achievement gains in Minnesota districts," which could be traced to PEG training.[115]

In a letter, Ian Keith, a St. Paul teacher and former head of the district's teachers union, wrote that as the district reduced suspensions, it did not replace them with other meaningful consequences for disruptive behavior. In the name of honoring cultural differences, it has condoned behaviors that can make it harder for other students to learn.[116]

Chong Thao, another St. Paul teacher, said that PEG itself was guilty of racial stereotyping, citing a PEG presenter who used national data to show Asian children achieving on par with white children, but ignoring the fact that most Asian children in St. Paul are from refugee and recent immigrant families.[117]

Thao rejected the view that teachers send students to the principal's office because of the student's race. "I think punctuality is not a cultural trait," said Thao, and, "I think respect is not a cultural trait."[118]

However, once misbehaving students are sent to the principal's office, little is done. Aaron Benner, the African-American teacher, recounted to *EAGnews* an incident when an African-American student punched another student in the face over the type of shoes he was wearing:

The principal said they were just playing. I'm like, wow, that's just so wrong. You're not trying to help these kids. You just don't want any of this to be recorded.[119]

Benner further recalled:

When you have to discipline a student of color, you know you're going to be questioned by an administrator, who is going to try to keep that student in class by any means necessary. So you just keep that kid in the classroom and try to keep a safe classroom. There's no learning being done.[120]

According to Benner, St. Paul students "are being used in some sort of social experiment where they are not being held accountable for their behavior." Safety, not teaching, had become the "number one concern."[121]

Parents have also been shocked and appalled at the chaos in the classroom resulting from the St. Paul district's policies.

Daeona Griffin, a parent of a second-grade student in a St. Paul elementary school, volunteered to sit in class to assist her son's teacher after several incidents of physical attacks on her son. She was shocked to find, "My second-grader's class is the most dysfunctional classroom I have ever witnessed with my own two eyes."[122]

According to Griffin, the class had six extreme behavior students. She saw these students punch the teacher, walk the hallways during class, and cause general disruption of the class so that it took the teacher an hour and half to read two pages. "It's too much," she bitterly observed.[123]

Griffin told the St. Paul publication *City Pages* that she thinks the teacher is in hell. She says that all the teacher can do is repeat herself, telling the same kids to sit down and show respect, over and over.[124]

Although her son has been suspended in the past, she is in favor of tough discipline policies. "He's a behavior kid, too," she says, and "I'm not ever going to deny my child needs reinforcement." Further, she notes that despite her two sons' academic problems, the schools "just pass the kids on" and they "just go on to the next grade."[125]

Ultimately, the real losers in this destruction of school learning environments have been the students who want to be in class and learn. David McGill, a science teacher at a St. Paul gifted-and-talented magnet school, said that an African-American fourth-grade bully had "significantly compromised an entire year of science instruction" for his classmates. Yet, McGill lamented that teachers and administrators had not disciplined the child because of the district policy.[126] In other words, in order to avoid appearing racist to one minority bully, the district was willing to sacrifice the learning of an entire class of students.

PEG's reach is nationwide, with contracts in more than 180 school districts as of 2015. To the extent that its anti-suspension, anti-discipline recommendations are being implemented, PEG is contributing to the chaos in schools across America.

Politicians are also making it more difficult to keep order in the classroom.

In 2015, New York City mayor Bill de Blasio implemented new requirements on the city's public schools making it much more difficult to suspend disruptive students. Analyzing data from the New York City school-climate survey, a Manhattan Institute study found that from 2013-14 to 2015-16, "more than half of schools saw a deterioration in mutual respect, and only a fifth saw an improvement, according to students." Further, "On physical fighting, gang activity, and drug use, three times as many schools saw a deterioration as saw an improvement, according to students."[127]

It must be emphasized that this deterioration is according to the students, who must interact with their peers, including the disruptive ones, all throughout the school day. In terms of the number of public schools where things had deteriorated:

> In 2015-16, for example, there were 154 more schools than in 2013-14 where more than half of students said that students did not respect one another (387 vs. 243); there were 46 more schools where 30+% of students reported frequent gang activity; there were 32 more schools where 30+% of students reported frequent drug/ alcohol use; there were 105 more schools where 30+% of students reported frequent physical fights; and there were 28 more schools where 30+% of teachers said that order and discipline were not maintained.[128]

Schools especially hard hit by de Blasio's anti-suspensions policies are those with high minority student populations: "According to students, schools that serve 90+% minority students saw the most significant deterioration in school climate under the de Blasio discipline reform – compared with schools serving a lower percentage of minority students." For example, fighting increased in half of the schools with high minority populations and mutual respect deteriorated in 58 percent of the high-minority schools.[129]

In 2015-16, New York City Public Schools meted out nearly 16,000 fewer suspensions than in 2013-14, with the result that more than 375,000 students attended a school "where a higher percentage of teachers reported that order and discipline were not maintained."[130]

The Manhattan Institute study concludes: "But standardized test scores are, fundamentally, a second-order concern." More important to parents and their children, "If we believe what students and teachers report, hundreds of thousands of students in New York City are now being educated in schools that are less respectful, less orderly, and more violent."[131] In view of these findings, "what we know now should alarm parents – and not only those in New York."[132]

Some schools, fed up with student behavior problems, are returning to tough suspension policies.

In 2016-17 at Harrisburg High School in Pennsylvania, 500 students have been given suspension notices for skipping at least a week's work of classes. Principal Lisa Love said that students often go to school but then skip class and loiter in hallways and other parts of the school.

"If you're not in class," said Love, "all you're here to do then is to wreak havoc upon the school and disrupt the work that we are trying to do here." Love says that the student class-skippers disrupt the school's "focus on student achievement."[133]

"We don't like to suspend," Love emphasized, but "we need to send the message that the value of education comes first." Her supportive school superintendent, Sybill Knight-Burney, said that the school's decision should serve as a "wake-up call" to the community.[134]

"In order for us to get different results, we have to do something different," said the superintendent, and, "We can't be doing the same old, same old, and complain when we're getting the same results."[135]

Principal Love and Superintendent Knight-Burney are ultimately protecting the interests of those students who want to go to school and go to class and learn. Sadly, however, the thinking and policies of Love and Knight-Burney are going against the overwhelming anti-suspension, anti-discipline tide in the nation's public schools.

Writing in the publication *City Journal*, Manhattan Institute senior fellow Heather Mac Donald said: "Protecting well-behaved students' ability to learn is a school's highest obligation, and it is destroyed when teachers lose the option of removing chronically disruptive students from class."[136]

Crimes by Teachers Against Students

Teachers are supposed to be one of the lines of protection for students. However, according to a recent study, sex crimes by teachers have reached shocking levels.

Terry Abbott, who served as chief of staff for U.S. Secretary of Education Rod Paige in President George W. Bush's administration, tracked media reports of sex crimes by teachers against students and found that in 2014 alone there were 781 reported sex crimes by teachers and other school employees.[137] That is an average of 15 students per week who were sexually victimized by school personnel. "That's an abhorrent rate," says Abbott, "and a trend that deserves far more attention from school leaders and policy makers."[138]

As shocking as the actual number of sex crimes is the skyrocketing increase in these crimes. In Texas, Abbott found "investigations into alleged inappropriate teacher-student relationships has grown by 27 percent over the past three years [from 2011 to 2014], to 179." In Kentucky in 2011 there were 25 reported sexual relationships between teachers and students. By 2014, that number had grown to 45. He reported "a surge" in Alabama, "where the state investigated 31 cases during the year ending July 2013, nearly triple the number it had investigated just four years earlier."[139]

The individual crimes make for lurid and appalling reading:

> A 14-year-old student in Florida wrote his cellphone number on a classroom chalkboard because he wanted a classmate he liked to call him. The student indeed was contacted – not by the girl but by his 32-year-old teacher. Within days, police said, the two were involved in a sexual relationship.

> In Pennsylvania, a 33-year-old teacher approached a 17 year-old student at a school dance and began flirting with him, police said. The married teacher then sent the student sexual text messages and photos, along with a video of herself performing lewd acts, according to news reports. The relationship escalated, and the teacher pleaded guilty last month to institutional sexual assault. [140]

Abbott said that in the late 1990s and early 2000s the cases of sex crimes by teachers against students "seemed rare." However, he says that social media and text messaging have been catalysts to the steep rise in such crimes. "Classroom sexual predators," he observes, "have been exploiting these new, unsupervised modes of communication to develop improper relationships with students out of sight of parents and principals." He points out that in 2014, "at least 281 school employees – 36 percent of those accused or convicted of an inappropriate relationship with a student – were reported to have used social media to start or continue those relationships."[141] Examples include:

> In Louisiana, a school vice principal was charged after allegedly soliciting nude pictures from a 15-year-old student on Facebook.
>
> Authorities said a 54-year-old Oregon teacher exchanged more than 1,800 text messages with a 16-year-old student, many of them sexually explicit, before the teacher was convicted and sentenced to prison in August.
>
> A 31-year-old Florida teacher was charged after police said she allegedly used Facebook to solicit sex from at least four students.
>
> A Pennsylvania math teacher offered a student extra credit if she texted him nude pictures. He was sentenced to prison for up to 23 months.[142]

Abbott rightfully says, "Policymakers and school leaders need to get tougher on these cases." Yet, many school districts are unable to fire teachers who commit sexual and other crimes because of restrictive union contracts.

Some states have responded to years of reports of teacher crimes with new laws.

In California in 2014, Governor Jerry Brown signed Assembly Bill 215, which created a separate expedited process to deal with teachers accused of "egregious misconduct," which includes specified sex, drug, and child abuse and neglect offenses. School districts now have more flexibility as to when to issue notices of suspension or dismissal, and hearings must be commenced within certain expedited time periods. Also, local education entities cannot enter into agreements to not report egregious misconduct to relevant state or federal authorities, and they cannot agree to remove complaints against, investigations into, and discipline for egregious misconduct from employee personnel files. [143]

While California's new law improves the state's teacher dismissal statutes, which have been criticized by a state court as imposing "a real and appreciable impact on students' fundamental right to equality of education," many question whether it goes far enough.[144]

For example, Schools Legal Services, a respected legal services consortium administered by the school superintendent of Kern County in Southern California, says of AB 215, "Is it enough?" The organization notes, "Of particular concern is that AB 215 narrowly defines egregious misconduct to the exclusion of other serious crimes (i.e., aggravated assault, armed robbery, etc.)."[145] Thus, a teacher could engage in behavior that most people would consider "egregious," but would not be subject to the new law because it is not covered under the law's list of specific crimes. Given this limitation, it is no surprise then that many teachers accused of misconduct are still not investigated quickly or have their cases adjudicated swiftly.

In Los Angeles in 2016, the publication *LA School Report* found that 181 school district employees "are being paid to essentially do nothing while awaiting internal investigations about alleged misconduct, while the district has to hire substitutes to do their jobs."[146]

Of the 181 employees, 144 were teachers and 37 were classified employees, such as teacher aides or playground assistants. These employees were "housed" in rooms where they could not do any work, call anyone, or work on a computer. They had to report to work and put in a full day, and then they could go home. Specifically, the publication found:

> Forty-five of the cases are more than a year old. Most of the cases (40 percent) involve sexual abuse or harassment allegations, 29 percent involve accusations of violence, and 13 percent involve "below standard performance." . . .

> Last year, the numbers totaled 174 employees—151 teachers and 23 classified employees—with 37 percent involving sexual harassment or abuse allegations and 32 percent cited for violent behavior.[147]

Los Angeles Unified School District chief financial officer Megan Reilly said the amount set aside for housing employees and paying for substitutes in the 2016-17 budget was an astounding $15 million. School board member Ref Rodriguez said $15 million "is too much, and we have to figure out how to keep moving that forward so that the taxpayers aren't paying for someone to sit in a room, and if they are innocent they should go back to the classrooms and the money should go back to our kids."[148]

Yet, as *LA School Report* notes, a succession of Los Angeles school superintendents have vowed to reduce the number of employees in "teacher jails," but "the numbers continue to grow."[149]

Los Angeles is not the only district which uses "teacher jails" to deal with misbehaving teachers. Up until 2010, New York City had 700 teachers in so-called "rubber rooms" where they were paid to do no work while awaiting adjudication for various crimes and misdeeds. However, that year the city's education department and the teachers union reached an agreement to close down the rubber rooms. Yet, according to Betsy Combier, a veteran paralegal who helps defend teachers, "No one pays any attention to the agreement."[150] According to a *New York Post* investigation:

> The [New York City's Department of Education] refused to say how many removed teachers and other tenured staffers remain in limbo, but sources estimate 200 to 400 get paid while awaiting disciplinary hearings. Their salaries total $15 million to $20 million a year.[151]

The teachers in the rubber rooms could collect their salaries for no work for years, says the newspaper:

> Several teachers on the payroll have been benched for up to five years due to a stunning bureaucratic breakdown. The 2010 deal required the independent arbitrators who conduct termination trials to issue a decision 30 days after a hearing, so that vindicated teachers could return to work and bad ones could be axed. But decisions still come months — or even years — late. The DOE says it can't enforce the rule.

"They're just letting me sit here," said a teacher removed from the classroom nearly five years ago on charges of physically abusing children, which he denies. His trial ended four years ago. He makes about $70,000 a year.[152]

If teachers commit crimes or engage in misconduct, and states and public school systems fail to address these issues adequately, then parents would be right to wonder about the safety of their children. Why keep one's children in systems that do not put an urgent priority on protecting them?

Safety and Choice

In St. Paul, Minnesota, Hmong children are the school district's largest ethnic group. Their test scores have lagged behind state averages by significant margins and they score lower on college entrance exams. Yet, it is the disruption in the classroom that has caused many Hmong parents and their children to flee the district. St. Paul teacher Koua Yang says that when Hmong parents see academic disruption they start to quietly pull their kids.[153] Yang, ruefully notes, "Why do we have to leave?"[154]

Many parents, however, faced with crime, safety, and school climate worries have limited or no recourse. Unless they can afford a safer private school or move to another safer area, they and their children are stuck with dangerous neighborhood public schools. There have been some proposals, however, to give parents whose children are endangered greater school options.

A report by the Independent Women's Forum proposes a Safety Opportunity Scholarship for children to use to transfer to the school of their choice:

> Parents with a reasonable apprehension for their children's safety, based on the experiences of their children and/or actual incidents-based statistics schools would be required to report, would be allowed to transfer them to safer schools of their choosing using a Safety Opportunity Scholarship. Scholarships would be worth the same amount students' current public schools receive and could be used at any public district, charter, or virtual school, as well as at any participating private school, within or beyond students' resident school districts.[155]

Other options include universal school choice programs, which make choice options available to all parents. For example, Nevada's recently-enacted education savings accounts program deposits state funding into individual accounts that parents can access to pay for specified education expenses, including private school tuition. Given that private schools have not been subject to the anti-discipline policies of the public schools, and given their better safety record, parents using an education savings account could choose to send their children to safer private schools.

School-choice tools can give children who have been victimized at their local public schools an opportunity to attend school and learn without fear and anxiety.

Indiana student Zaya Lumumba had attended public schools in the town of Speedway, which is outside Indianapolis. Although Speedway's public schools are generally well performing, Zaya said that bullies in school had picked on her. Luckily for Zaya, Indiana has a school voucher program that gives school-choice scholarships to low- and middle-income students that they can use to help pay for private-school tuition. According to the *Indianapolis Star:*

> With the help of a school voucher, Zaya left her public school for Providence Cristo Rey [private Catholic school]. And she is flourishing, recording a top-grade point average and getting a head start on her dream to be a doctor through a work study at a hospital.[156]

Zaya's experience shows that student achievement is often connected to the school environment in which students are placed. A safe, peaceful and welcoming environment fosters learning, while a dangerous, threatening and dysfunctional environment does not. John Elcesser, executive director of the Indiana Non-Public Education Association, observes:

> The biggest place [that proves results] is ask the parents: How is your student doing here as opposed to where they were before? Are they performing better academically? Does it feel like a better fit for them in the environment that they're in, in terms of school climate and culture? The whole idea of choice is to put the parents in power in terms of making the decisions."[157]

Zaya believes that if she had stayed at her previous Speedway public school, she would have gotten into trouble because of her conflicts with bullies. Now, at her new private school, she says:

> Everybody knows me. They know me as goofy Zaya. I just like the feeling that I can talk to people, and it's just a happy feeling when you get to laugh in the hallways.[158]

The millions of student victims in the federal crime statistics and the many millions more who are victimized by bullying, harassment and intimidation could have a life like Zaya if they and their parents had a school-choice tool like the one Zaya's parents used to send her to Cristo Rey. A better school does not always mean a higher achieving school. Sometimes a better school could mean a safer school.

Chapter Three: Fiscal Mismanagement

Fiscal Mismanagement

As any business person will tell you, how a company's money is managed has as much to do with success as having a good product. For example, consumers loved Krispy Kreme doughnuts, but poor management sent the company into a tailspin in the first decade of the 2000s. The same is true of public school systems, where fiscal mismanagement can help destroy learning in the classroom.

The examples of mismanagement in school districts are legion and extend from coast to coast.

The Los Angeles Unified School District is the second largest school district in the nation. In 2015, a panel of luminaries that included a former state superintendent of public instruction, a former state attorney general and state treasurer, a former chief financial officer for the University of California, and other experts informed the district that it was facing a looming, long-term deficit that could push the district into bankruptcy. The panel estimated that from 2017-18 to 2019-20, the three-year deficit could total about $1.4 billion.[159]

The panel was convened by then-district superintendent Ramon Cortines in response to critics, including the district's own chief financial officer, who said that that the district could not afford contract agreements with employee unions.[160] It should be pointed out that while some financial factors are out of the control of decision-makers, how contracts are negotiated and approved is totally within the control of the elected school board.

The report said pointedly that while the district had experienced some "near-term successes," these positives would be "very difficult to maintain and expand in the face of very stark demographic and financial forecasts."[161]

The Los Angeles school district is experiencing declining enrollment, yet, according to the *Los Angeles Times*, "the district's number of employees has, so far, not matched that decline."[162] Again, keeping the number of employees high is a decision within the power and discretion of the school board, and the panel recommended reducing staffing in line with declining enrollment.[163]

One would think that the Los Angeles school board would take strong action when presented with such a harrowing scenario. Indeed, the board did take action, but not in the way that any responsible steward of the public's tax dollars would.

In August 2016, less than a year after the panel of experts delivered its fiscal warning to the district, the school board voted unanimously to incur a huge new expense. As the *Los Angeles Times* reported, "Los Angeles school officials constantly warn of a looming financial crisis, but they've taken on a new expense as if there were money to spare: health benefits for about 4,200 more part-time workers."[164] The cost of the new benefits is estimated to be $16 million per year, which Susan Shelley, a columnist writing in the *Los Angeles Daily News*, says is "money that the district doesn't have."[165]

Why would the board vote to add on a huge new expense in the midst of dire fiscal crisis? Politics, of course:

> The Board of Education last week voted to extend the benefits to teacher assistants, playground aides, and others. All are members of Local 99 of the Service Employees International Union, which is expected to be a significant player in the March 2017 elections. The union's win comes as the season nears for candidate endorsements.[166]

Despite looming bankruptcy, the politics-driven board voted for the new benefits to part-time employees, without any discussion, even though overly generous benefit packages are one key reason for the district's pending fiscal doom. The *Los Angeles Times* quoted the principal author of this book saying: "The school system does not exist as an expensive employment program for adults. Diverting money from the classroom to new benefits for part-time workers demonstrates that the LAUSD school board has its priorities mixed up."[167]

Yet, the political influence of the Service Employees International Union has overcome all rational fiscal policy thinking:

> The union said that negotiations over the additional coverage began in 2014, and it insisted the action was unrelated to elections. Even so, Local 99 has long proved a reliable and generous supporter of incumbents, who have delivered through actions that supporters said also benefited students.

In 2014, the board put the district out front in a national movement to raise the minimum wage to $15 an hour. Some Local 99 members' hourly wages nearly doubled.

After the Sandy Hook school shooting in 2012, the district hired hundreds of unarmed security aides — all union members.

In 2007, the district granted benefits to part-time cafeteria workers, throwing the cafeteria budget into a deficit that must be supplemented from the general fund. Later, food workers' jobs and hours expanded when the district began requiring that federally funded breakfasts be brought to all students in their classrooms, whether they ate them or not.[168]

The panel-of-experts report pointedly said that the district spent too much on cafeteria operations.[169]

The district's superintendent, Michelle King, signed off on the deal with the union, despite knowing full well the fiscal consequences and eventual impact on classrooms across the district. King said, "the district will have to identify additional balancing strategies" and make "program adjustments." As columnist Susan Shelley notes, "That delicate language means cuts to education."[170] In other words, the interest of the powerful union was more important than the interests of the children, for whom the district supposedly exists in the first place.

Who can blame parents if they would like their children to leave a school district that places lower importance on their needs than on the agendas of wealthy special interests. As Susan Shelley concludes:

> Education in California is being looted, which is bad enough, but worse is that the looting is perpetuated by cutting education and then showing voters the bleeding so they'll vote for higher taxes.
>
> The students suffer because the crisis, though manufactured, is genuine. That's the way the deal was negotiated.[171]

The consequences of fiscal insanity cannot be imagined away – the piper must be paid. So, less than four months after voting for the new benefit package for part-time workers, the Los Angeles school district was forced to inform Los Angeles County and the state of California that it may not be able to meet its financial obligations because of a cumulative deficit of nearly $1.5 billion through the 2018-19 school year.[172]

The district's chief financial officer Megan Reilly said, "We have to identify programs to bring down the deficits."[173] In other words, cuts will have to be made that will undoubtedly impact students.

Also ominous, Reilly said that an additional unfunded liability of $13 billion for health benefits is not included in the calculations.

School board member Richard Vladovic said, "We are hoping for the best, and advocate for the best, but if we don't plan for the worst, bad things happen and who suffers, but our children."[174] Yet, who caused this mess in the first place?

It was Mr. Vladovic and his colleagues on the board who leapt at the chance to do the bidding of powerful special interests to the detriment of the district's students. But now, when presented with the bill for his profligacy and that of his board colleagues, he worries about the suffering of "our children."

Los Angeles is not an anomaly when it comes to fiscal mismanagement. Chicago is the third-largest school district in the nation and its financial woes rival those of Los Angeles.

According to a Manhattan Institute report, the Chicago Public Schools (CPS), like LAUSD, faces "shrinking student enrollment coupled with rigid labor costs and escalating legacy pension costs," which combine to "cause considerable budgetary strain."[175]

Like Los Angeles, Chicago's troubles are a tale of too much spending and too little revenue. From 2001 to 2015, inflation-adjusted spending per pupil increased by 37 percent, while inflation-adjusted district pension contributions increased by an incredible 618 percent. In contrast, inflation-adjusted revenue rose by just 22 percent. Stating the ultra-obvious, CPS CEO Forest Claypool said, "CPS is facing a budgetary crisis."[176]

The Manhattan Institute report observes, "Because the majority of a school district's spending is on salaries and benefits, there is only so much that can be cut elsewhere."[177] Thus, while overall per-pupil spending, which includes labor costs, has gone up significantly, the report says, "from 2001-15, annual per-pupil inflation-adjusted spending on textbooks declined by 36 percent, and spending on classroom and other supplies fell by nearly 60 percent."[178] In other words, the impact of Chicago's fiscal mismanagement fell hardest on its children.

As in Los Angeles, Chicago's parents would be right to wonder why they should stay in a system that devalues their children.

Chicago, at least, is responsible for most of its own teacher pension costs. For the rest of Illinois, there is a perverse incentive built into the pension system. According to Michael Lucci of the Illinois Policy Institute:

> Local school boards decide the pay increases that determine the final value of teacher pensions. However, state government pays for those pensions through the Teachers' Retirement System, or TRS. This gives local school boards an incentive to boost the value of teacher pensions to appease local teaching staffs while passing the cost to taxpayers somewhere else. Illinois taxpayers are unwittingly footing the bill for inflated contracts across the state through this financial scheme, which benefits teachers and local school board members.
>
> But the system is set up to incentivize local school boards to behave this way – they get to give out expensive benefits to people in their district while essentially taxing other districts to pay for it. Why not tax people in other districts to give perks to teachers in your district?[179]

Lucci observes that the third-party payer structure in Illinois, where state taxpayers are responsible for local teacher pension costs, leads to "pension spiking," where teachers are given big salary increases before retirement to boost their pensions. He cites "a 10-year teachers' contract in Palatine (that) includes four consecutive years of 6 percent raises before teachers retire, bumping a teacher with an $80,000 salary up to a $101,000 salary in his or her last four years." The final pension, he says, for which the state pays, "is based on an average of these last four years of salary."[180]

Such perverse incentives have led to a catastrophic situation for the teacher pension fund in Illinois. "Only $45 billion of assets are on hand to cover a liability currently at $119 billion," says Lucci, which "leaves a $73.4 billion debt hole in the [teacher retirement system] pension fund."[181] He notes that the interest alone on the debt is $5.1 billion per year, and "Illinois is not even covering the interest payment, meaning the debt will continue increasing for the foreseeable future."[182]

In Los Angeles, when faced with fiscal disaster, district and union leaders urged Californians to vote for higher state taxes to help pay for the contracts they have negotiated. In Illinois, Lucci says, "school board members can get the benefits of happy teachers and better labor relations with the teachers union by giving teachers this perk paid for by other people." Since the costs are passed on to state taxpayers, these school board members "do not face local accountability when they juice pensions because local taxpayers don't directly pay for those pensions."[183]

Another large school district facing a self-made fiscal disaster is Baltimore. In January 2017, district officials revealed that the district had a massive $130 million deficit, which amounted to a staggering 10 percent of the district's $1.3 billion budget. Officials said that the reasons for the deficit included expensive teacher union contracts that hiked teacher salaries, providing full-day pre-kindergarten when the state of Maryland only requires half a day, and pouring money into capital projects. The school board and district officials made these bad decisions voluntarily without anyone putting a gun to their heads.[184]

The impact of the district's mismanagement of tax dollars will greatly impact students. Baltimore city schools

CEO Sonja Santelises said that arts, career technology, and enrichment classes will be cut and class size will increase by as much as 10 students per class. "This is going to hit everything kids love about coming to school," said Santelises.[185]

Yet, the fault for this hit to students lies with the adults in the school district who spent money that the district did not have and who relied on budget gimmickry and failed to address the structural deficit in the budget. According to *The Baltimore Sun*:

> Santelises said that tactics used to close budget gaps half this size in prior years, such as superficial funding cuts and paying for reoccurring expenses with one-time funding sources, did not work because they were not financially sustainable.[186]

"This isn't something that randomly happened to us," said Santelises. "What we've seen is the district has closed deficits every year, with a series of one-time fixes." Baltimore school board Chair Marnell Cooper admitted, "It's going to keep happening until we change the structure."[187]

On the other side of the country in December 2016, San Diego Unified School District officials announced a $117 million deficit, about 9 percent of the district's $1.3 billion budget. The size of the budget deficit is twice the size of the money budgeted for books and supplies in the district.[188]

As in Baltimore, a significant contributing factor to the budget deficit was an expensive teacher union contract.

Over the past several years, San Diego school board members have voted for a series of increases to teacher salaries. By July of 2015, teacher compensation had increased by 10 percent since the start of the 2014-

15 school year. Subsequently, the board voted in 2016 to ratify a contract with the San Diego Education Association that will give teachers an across-the-board 4 percent raise. The deal opened up the way for other school employees to receive similar raises based on a longstanding "me too clause."[189]

The raises in the new teacher union contract will add $30 million in added costs to the district in 2016-17 and will add at least $50 million more in 2018-19.[190] In addition, in 2016-17, the district contributed $124 million to the California State Teachers' Retirement System, versus $75.7 million two years previously.

The school board approved the expensive teacher union contract even though it had spent down the district's reserve to a minimum and had been warned about the pending fiscal disaster.

Indeed, the publication *Voice of San Diego* observed, "San Diego Unified officials are used to spending money faster than they receive it, which has resulted in budget shortfalls totaling millions of dollars each year."[191] The district dealt with previous deficits by employing stopgap measures such as selling off district-owned real estate. But now the piper must be paid, and San Diego students are the ones who will suffer from the poor fiscal management of adult decision-makers.

To try and balance the 2016-17 budget, special education and early education programs were cut. Some preschool programs have started charging parents for preschool classes. Despite these cuts, the San Diego County Office of Education issued a letter saying it was "extremely concerned" that the district would be able to reduce its spending adequately in upcoming fiscal years.[192]

When there is disastrous fiscal mismanagement in school districts, one oft-used response is for state governments to take over the failing local district.

In New Mexico, the state Public Education Department (PED) took over the scandal-ridden Española School District. According to a media report, "PED Secretary Hannah Skandera issued a letter . . . to the Española school board pointing to financial mismanagement in the district over the past five years."[193] The report says that the secretary "will control all funds under the board's control and act as the fiscal agent, meaning she will take whatever actions she deems necessary to ensure the district complies with the law."[194]

Large districts like Philadelphia, Detroit, and Newark, plus smaller districts around the country have, at one time or another, been taken over their respective state governments over the last couple of decades. While some of these takeovers have corrected the fiscal problems of the districts, student academic performance often remains stubbornly low. Mike Petrilli of the Fordham Institute describes the problem with the state-takeover solution:

> What typically will happen is the state will simply replace the superintendent with someone they choose. If nothing else changes – the central office stays the same, all of the systems, curriculum, all of those reasons that the system is failing in the first place – then [the superintendent] doesn't necessarily make the radical changes you need to see for radically different performance.[195]

Indeed, according to a Pew Charitable Trust report on state takeovers, "there is no indication that any particular system for governing urban school districts is superior to another in improving long-term academic performance."[196]

The bottom line is that fiscal mismanagement by school districts can have a terrible impact on students in the classroom. This mismanagement is widespread around the country. The nuclear option of governance change – state takeover – has a checkered record and often does not result in better student outcomes. Thus, parents and their children should be able to escape these fiscal bad actors through school choice options.

Chapter Four:
Sexualization of
the Classroom

Sexualization of the Classroom

Nothing causes the tempers of parents to flare more than sex-related policies promulgated by school districts. Sometimes the districts feel pressured by the judiciary or state and federal governments to push the sexual envelope, but other times they make decisions that are totally within their discretion.

In Pennsylvania, parents of a student have filed a lawsuit against the Boyertown Area School District over the district's transgender policies.[197]

The Philadelphia Inquirer reported that the lawsuit alleges that parents and students were not notified by the school district that it was allowing transgendered students to use restrooms and locker rooms matching their chosen identify, and that the district "secretly opened" its sex-specific restrooms and locker rooms to students of the opposite sex. Further, school officials allegedly told the student, essentially, to live with the changes:

According to the filing, the student complained to school officials, who informed him that students who "subjectively identify themselves as the opposite sex" can choose which locker room they use. When the student twice asked school officials to protect his privacy, he was told he must "tolerate" it and make changing with students of the opposite sex as "natural" as can be, the suit said.[198]

The lawsuit alleges sexual harassment under federal Title IX; violation of the fundamental right to bodily privacy under the U.S. Constitution; and violation of a state privacy law.[199] Randall Wenger, chief counsel for the Harrisburg-based Independence Law Center and one of the lawyers for the parents and the student, stated:

No school should rob any student of his legally protected personal privacy. We trust that our children won't be forced into emotionally vulnerable situations like this when they are in the care of our schools because it's a school's duty to protect and respect the bodily privacy and dignity of all students. In this case, school officials are clearly ignoring that duty.[200]

The Boyertown Area School District responded to the lawsuit by acknowledging that the Trump administration had rescinded Obama-era federal guidelines allowing transgendered students to use the bathrooms and locker rooms of their choice. The district also admitted that the state of Pennsylvania did not have a specific law addressing transgender students and bathroom and locker room access.

However, the district defended its policy by pointing to a recent federal court ruling in Pennsylvania.[201]

In February 2017, a federal district court judge ruled in favor of three Pennsylvania transgender students, issuing a preliminary injunction allowing them to use the bathroom corresponding with their chosen identity.[202] It should be pointed out that the ruling is not the final decision in the case, but is merely a preliminary ruling that is in effect as the case proceeds through the judicial process. The ultimate ruling may turn out not to favor the transgender students and their claims of civil rights violations.

Other school districts, however, are not forced to enact particular sex-related policies, but have the discretion to do so. Curriculum is a good example.

In 2014, the school district in Fremont, California, which is in the eastern portion of the San Francisco Bay Area, tried to introduce a ninth-grade health textbook that, according to the *San Francisco Chronicle,* included "drawings of sexual anatomy; mentions vibrators, oral sex and bondage; and information on how to buy and use a condom."[203]

The textbook, entitled *Your Health Today* and which some Texas districts also used, included a section addressing online dating, with a guide to several dating websites. Various female sterilization procedures are discussed. Also, the book discussed sexual techniques that go beyond simply explaining how babies are created.

For example, the book described so-called "erotic touch," which it said, "is a sensual form of communication that can elicit feelings of tenderness and affection as well as sexual feelings." Further, erotic touch "is an important part of foreplay, touching that increases sexual arousal and precedes sexual intercourse."[204]

The book goes on to say that while women place more emphasis on kissing "for beginning and sustaining a relationship," men "may place more emphasis on kissing as a means to advance to oral sex or intercourse."[205] Sexual fantasies are defined as "mental images, scenarios, and daydreams imagined to initiate sexual arousal." These fantasies "range from simple images to complicated erotic stories."[206]

The book also included elaborate dating and sexual scenarios involving college students. Remember, this book was intended for ninth graders. One so-called "Life Story" involved two sexually active college students:

> Madison and Tomas were both sophomores and had been dating each other exclusively for a year. They met their freshman year and almost instantly bonded. Madison had some sexual experiences before college, but Tomas was her first real boyfriend. Madison was shy and Tomas was outgoing – qualities that they both liked about each other. A lot of their friends hooked up with other people at parties and had casual sex, but Madison and Tomas were happy with their exclusive relationship. Their friends thought they were a little boring and "old fashioned," but also envied them for being satisfied with their relationship.

> For spring semester of sophomore year, Tomas was planning to attend a study abroad program in Italy. A week before he was leaving, he told Madison that he wanted to be open to other relationships while they were apart. He said he cared about her but saw the trip as a chance to find out if "they were meant to be together." He

wanted to have a new experience, including sexual experiences, if they came along, and he didn't want to feel like he was cheating on her while he was away.

Madison was caught by surprise. She said okay, but only because she didn't know what else to say. She felt confused and rejected. After Tomas left, she figured she might as well use this time to explore new relationships herself – at least it would help get her mind off Tomas. She started partying more with her friends and tried to cast off her shy persona. She would have a few drinks (or more) and make herself dance and flirt. She was surprised to find that she got a lot of attention. It made her feel attractive and popular – and like she was getting back at Tomas. The first time a guy made it clear he wanted to hook up with her, she turned him down, but the next time she accepted. She found it exciting, but also awkward, especially when the alcohol wore off. She enjoyed the sex but missed the intimacy she shared with Tomas – the talking, laughing, and sense of closeness and trust. She was also dismayed that the guy she hooked up with didn't call or email her. She felt rejected all over again and dreaded running into him on campus.

Tomas sent her messages on Facebook with upbeat descriptions of all the fun things he was doing and said that he missed her. Neither of them brought up the topic of seeing other people or hooking up. Reading messages from Tomas, Madison realized how much she missed him and how hooking up was not helping her with her feelings. In fact, it was making her feel worse. She decided to ask Tomas to clarify his feeling about her so she could make some decision about her own actions. She also decided that hooking up was not for her, at least for right now.

Do you think that Madison's experience of hooking up is typical? What other experiences do you think that people have with this practice? Do you think that women suffer more than men after a hook up? If so, why?

Where does hooking up fit into your personal value system, if at all?[207]

This story brings up a whole litany of concerns. Why are ninth graders made to grapple with the sexual behavior of college students? The entire scenario is laid out in an amoral landscape, where the only things that matter are the personal feelings of the individuals involved. If Tomas enjoys hooking up, should he continue to do so simply because he likes it? Despite the bulleted questions at the end of the story, what is the purpose of including such a story at all?

Not surprisingly, the textbook ignited outrage among parents in the school district, despite the socially liberal reputation of the San Francisco Bay Area. Hundreds of people signed a petition to urge the Fremont school board to rescind its decision to use the textbook in ninth-grade health classes.

"I feel that it's not age appropriate for these kids," worried Asfia Ahmed, a mother of a student. "I have read the book from first page to last," she said, "and most pages talk about college kids." "It doesn't relate to these [ninth graders] at all."[208]

The textbook is listed as a college health textbook on bookseller sites, but the *San Francisco Chronicle* noted that district officials claimed that the ninth graders needed the information well before they got to college, arguing that it is too late once they get there.[209]

Fremont Unified School District board of education president Lara Calvert-York admitted that the textbook talked about masturbation, but defended it by saying that such topics are part of California's state standards. "We really want [the ninth graders] to have a safe place to get facts about their bodies and how to handle things and how they need to be mature to deal with these things."[210]

School district health teachers unanimously chose the textbook from a group of six that were evaluated and reviewed. Following the recommendation of the teachers, the school board adopted the book in June 2014.[211]

While teachers, district officials, and school board members marched in lockstep, someone forgot to tell the parents because they had a very different view about whether their ninth graders should be asked to handle a college sex-ed textbook.

Parents called the book too explicit, and called the depictions offensive and not necessary for their children. Overall, many parents complained that the textbook failed to reflect the family and cultural values of the community.[212]

Ms. Ahmed told the *New York Daily News*, "The main problem is that this book treats the kids as adults and the content is adult."[213]

Eventually, the Fremont school board backed off from the textbook. However, for parents across California, the potential for future such occurrences are strong because state standards seem to support the push coming from educators.

"The teachers felt here is what California requires, here are the standards, this is the best match for it," said Fremont superintendent James Morris to NBC's Today Show.[214] And moves by state lawmakers have continued to push the sex-ed envelope.

In October 2015, Governor Jerry Brown signed the California Healthy Youth Act, which "require(s) school districts to ensure that all pupils in grades 7-12 . . . receive comprehensive sexual health education and HIV prevention education."[215] Previously, districts were only required to provide HIV-prevention education once in middle school and once in high school.[216]

The new law opens the door to an ideological sexual agenda in California's public schools. Districts are now in the process of adopting controversial curricula aligned to the dictates of the new law.

In the town of Cupertino, located in California's Silicon Valley south of San Francisco, the Cupertino Union School District leadership pushed for the local school board to adopt a new middle-school curriculum that would meet the 2015 state law's requirement "to provide pupils with the knowledge and skills necessary to protect their sexual and reproductive health from HIV and other sexually transmitted infections and from unintended pregnancy (and) provide pupils with the knowledge and skills they need to develop healthy attitudes concerning adolescent growth and development, body image, gender, sexual orientation, relationships, marriage and family."[217] Of course, "healthy attitudes" are to be determined not by parents, but by curriculum developers and the textbook industry, state policymakers, school district officials, and teachers.

The district formed a Human Growth and Development Task Force in fall 2016, made up mostly of teachers, administrators and other school employees. The Task Force recommended a curriculum called "Teen Talk Middle School," which is published by Health Connected.

The district's director of math and science, Hans Barber, told the *San Jose Mercury News* that it was important to adopt the new curriculum as soon as possible to be in compliance with the new state law. In addition, he said that the district had already received a letter from the American Civil Liberties Union urging the board to adopt a curriculum aligned with the state law or else face potentially costly litigation.[218]

Perhaps most damning of all, teacher Kristina Everhardt told the CBS-TV affiliate in San Francisco that, "One of our movies literally that I showed in seventh grade last year implied that boys were only looking for sex and girls needed to protect their virginity."[219] That a public school teacher is shocked by the idea that middle-school girls should protect their virginity shows just how out of touch teachers can be with the legitimate views and concerns of the parents of the children they are supposed to educate.

In contrast, the new curriculum adopted by the Task Force opened the floodgates to all manner of sexual activity, which outraged parents:

> The issue for many parents was the graphic nature of the material, and how far is too far when it comes to sex ed in middle school. The proposed curriculum included descriptions of vaginal, oral, and anal sex, along with material on homosexuality.[220]

Parent Sri Sarma, who had reviewed the proposed material, called the curriculum "explicit" and "extremely provocative," and concluded, "It was written with too much suggestion." Another parent, Muni Madhdhipatla, concurred saying that the curriculum was "too graphic and descriptive, and it's leading kids in a certain way." Mr. Madhdhipatla asked, "My best question to them is, are we teaching to perform or inform?"[221]

The parent backlash culminated in a March 2017 school board meeting which was packed with roughly 150 parents who carried signs with messages such as "Over-exposure damages" and "Do not put adult ideas in my child's head." In addition, more than 4,300 people signed an online petition opposing the new curriculum.[222]

After hearing from more than 50 speakers, the Cupertino school board voted 2 to 2 on the new sex curriculum, killing its implementation. While the vote was a victory for local parents, the question arises as to what would those parents have done if the board had voted to implement the sex curriculum. They could have organized and voted out the pro-curriculum board members, but in the interim their children would have been exposed to a curriculum that they vehemently opposed. However, if they had access to a school-choice tool, such as a voucher or an education savings account, they could immediately take their children out from the public schools and place them in private schools that better reflected their values.

Chapter Five:
Religious Bias

Religious Bias

Most Americans have an inherent instinct for fairness and balance. Whatever their own personal beliefs, most people want to hear both sides of an argument and the multiplicity of views that weave together the great American fabric. That inherent fairness applies to religion as well as politics.

Just as parents do not like teacher and school officials to favor one political candidate over another, so parents oppose the promotion of one religious faith over another. Yet, in public schools across America, teaching, curricula and policies seem intended to disfavor Christianity and favor other religious faiths.

In New Jersey in February 2017, Libby Hilsenrath and Nancy Gayer, two parents with seventh-grade sons in a local public school in the town of Chatham, addressed the local school board complaining that the instruction and curriculum at the school promoted the teaching of the tenets of Islam, while censoring and excluding similar teaching of the tenets of Christianity.

Ms. Gayer told the Chatham Board of Education that several years earlier, a teacher told her son that the inclusion of a short quote from the Bible in his PowerPoint presentation "belongs in Sunday school, not in the classroom." The Bible line, "he who lends to the poor, lends to the Lord," was included in her son's presentation on collecting warm clothes for underprivileged children.[223]

The teacher also claimed that the computer would not allow the presentation to be shown to the class. Ms. Gayer then went to the school district superintendent who told her that the teacher's actions were correct and in accordance with the district's policy of prohibiting "proselytizing" in the classroom.[224] Yet, the district's anti-proselytizing policy evidently did not apply to the district's own World Cultures and Geography curriculum.

Seventh-grade student at Chatham Middle School, including the sons of Ms. Hilsenrath and Ms. Gayer, were taught the tenets of Islam, including through the use of an animated video entitled "The 5 Pillars." In the video, a Muslim boy teaches his non-Muslim friend the 5 Pillars of Islam, which are faith, prayer, charity, fasting and pilgrimage. During the video, a subtitle of bright, multi-colored words of various shapes pronounces a form of the Islamic conversion creed: "There is no god except Allah and Prophet Muhammad is His messenger." The video ends with the Muslim boy inviting his non-Muslim friend to join him at the mosque for noon-day prayers.[225]

Ms. Hilsenrath showed other course material to the school board that could be viewed as proselytizing for Islam, including a video providing an introduction to Islam. The video contained quotes from the Koran such as "And they say: Be Jews and Christians, then ye shall be rightly guided. Say (unto them, O Muhammad) Nay, but (we follow) the religion of Abraham, the upright, and he was not of the idolaters" and "Lo, we have sent thee (O Muhammad) with the truth, a bringer of glad tidings and warner."[226]

The seventh-graders were never given similar instruction in other world religions, such as Christianity, Judaism, etc. Both mothers said that there is nothing wrong with being taught the tenets of world religions, but there is a problem when only one religion is taught to the exclusion of others, and especially when a brief line from the Bible is enough to squelch a student's class presentation.[227]

The school district superintendent, Michael LaSusa, refused to eliminate the course and argued that it is part of the New Jersey curriculum core content standards to teach religions of the world.[228] However, the course in question only discussed the tenets of Islam.

The two mothers have been denounced as bigots, xenophobes, and Islamophobes in social media. Yet, they do not seek to bar the teaching of the tenets of Islam, but simply want the course to teach the tenets of other religions as well. As Nancy Gayer said, "It's just not fair that within this unit of study the Chatham school district taught one religion to the exclusion of all others, and for the community to be so unkind and unwelcoming towards us, just for having raised legitimate questions as parents."[229]

Ms. Hilsenrath said that the Middle East and North Africa section of the World Cultures and Geography class only discusses Islam, despite the fact that Christianity and Judaism have deep roots in the region. When she asked about this discrepancy, she said that she was told that the two other religions are discussed in other classes. Superintendent LaSusa claimed that Christianity is discussed throughout the curriculum, especially in the study of U.S. history. However, Ms. Hilsenrath countered saying, "when it comes to teaching other religions to this level, it's not done."[230]

Similar incidents have occurred in other states. In Maryland, John Kevin Wood and his wife Melissa, who are Christians, objected to the assignments in their daughter's 11th-grade World History class at La Plata High School, which they charged unfairly favored the teaching of Islam over other religions such as Christianity.

According to a 2016 federal lawsuit filed by Mr. and Mrs. Wood against the Charles County Public Schools, the school board, and various school officials, the school spent two weeks teaching the tenets of Islam, but only one day teaching about Christianity. The school did not inform students or parents of the extensive teaching of Islam in the course syllabus. Also, the syllabus failed to mention that the school used two different textbooks – one that could be taken home by students that did not extensively cover Islam, and another that was kept at school that did extensively cover Islam.[231]

In the course, according to the Woods, students, including their daughter, were required to profess statements on the teachings and beliefs of Islam in written worksheets as graded homework assignments. For example, students were required to profess the *Shahada*, which says, "There is no god but Allah and Muhammad is the messenger of Allah."[232]

Like in the New Jersey case of Lisa Hilsenrath and Nancy Gaynor, the Woods' daughter was instructed from the text of the Koran and had to learn and recite the Five Pillars of Islam. Course assignments included biased and subjective statement such as "most Muslims' faith is stronger than the average Christian."[233] School officials said that the Woods' daughter would receive zeros on assignments not completed, even if they violated their religious beliefs.[234] The daughter continued to refuse to complete the assignments, was given zeros, and resulting in a lower course grade.[235]

In contrast to the in-depth coverage of Islam, its holy text, and its key beliefs, the one-day coverage of Christianity failed to cover any portion of the Bible, including key belief statements such as the Ten Commandments. Instead, the lawsuit charged, the class included disparaging remarks about Christianity and the Pope.[236]

When Mr. Wood called the school vice principal to say that the school's failure to address his family's concerns would result in pursuing their complaints through lawyers and the media, the school responded by banning Mr. Woods from coming onto campus.[237]

In their lawsuit, the Woods note that the school district provides alternative assignments and accommodations to students of other religions. For instance, the district's middle schools allow accommodations to be made for Islamic students who cannot satisfy certain physical education requirements due to wearing religious clothing, such as a hijab.[238] In other words, by not accommodating the Woods' daughter and her sincerely held religious beliefs, the school district engaged in a clear double standard:

> Defendants, however, do not treat Christianity in the same manner as Islam. Defendants do not require students to profess or write out faith statements of Christianity, including creeds associated with Christianity. In fact, Defendants teach about Christianity in a disparaging manner and do not require students to learn any tenets of Christianity or Judaism.[239]

Once again, the issue is one of fairness and balance. If these schools taught about each religion in the same way, allocating equivalent time and instruction, then even strong Christians like the Woods would have much less about which to complain.

As the Woods lawsuit pointed out, the U.S. Supreme Court has held that public schools should not promote a certain religion over others: "School sponsorship of a religious message is impermissible because it sends the ancillary message to member of the audience who are non-adherents 'that they are outsiders, . . . and an accompanying message to adherents they are insiders. '"[240] Favoring any religion, in this case Islam, violates the First Amendment to the U.S. Constitution, which forbids the establishment of a particular religion by government, and which also forbids government from compelling speech from individuals in violation of their free speech rights.[241]

In May 2017, six San Diego parents, the Citizens for Quality Education, and the San Diego Asian Americans for Equality Foundation sued the San Diego Unified School District in federal court over the district's special anti-Islamophobia program. The program includes providing training and materials for school staff, creating "safe spaces" for Muslim students, and establishing a partnership with the controversial Council on American-Islamic Relations (CAIR).[242] No comparable program exists for students of any other religion.

Under the program, Muslim students could complain about bias and bullying to CAIR, which would then file a report with the district.[243]

Frank Xu, president of the San Diego Asian Americans for Equality, commented, "Students of all faiths face daily bullying, but instead of protecting all religious students, the school district has selected Muslim students to receive special protection and resources."[244]

The suit contends, among other things, that by establishing the program, the district is favoring one religion over others, which violates the U.S. Constitution's First Amendment.

At some public schools, unfortunately, there is no even-handedness in the teaching of religion. Faced with such lack of balance, parents should have the school-choice tools that will allow them to access education options that that fit their values.

Conclusion

Conclusion

There is no doubt that how much a child achieves academically will have a huge impact on his or her life.

For instance, data from the California Community Colleges Chancellor's Office show that 70 percent of freshmen students who come to community college prepared for college-level work eventually attain a degree or certificate. However, less than 40 percent of freshmen students who need to take remedial courses in math or English eventually receive a degree or certificate.

Yet, as this book amply illustrates, there are many other reasons, besides academic achievement, that could influence whether parents wish to keep their children in a local public school.

A public school might have decent test scores, but if parents feel their children are being politically indoctrinated; are at risk of being victimized by other students or teachers; are being shortchanged because of mismanagement by school officials; or are having their basic value system overturned, then parents and their children should have the right and the tools to exit the public school system for educational alternatives that better meet their needs and preferences.

Writing in *The Federalist*, education policy analyst Inez Feltscher Stepman observes, "equally important to how well American students learn is what they learn."[245]

There is an exploding realization among many parents that the now dominant progressive ideology of the public schools is incompatible with their bedrock beliefs.

Polling data on the beliefs of the young Millennial generation underscore the impact the ideologized and politicized instruction they received in their public schools.

A recent study by YouGov found that nearly equal proportions of Millennials support socialism as support capitalism.[246] Of those who have heard of him, 1 out of 4 Millennials have a favorable opinion of Vladimir Lenin. Even worse, a larger proportion of Millennials believe that more people were killed by the administration of George W. Bush than were killed by Joseph Stalin.[247]

Perhaps most shocking, only 25 percent of millennials believe that living in a democracy is essential, down from 75 percent in their grandparents' generation.[248]

Marion Smith, executive director of the Victims of Communism Memorial Foundation, recently wrote that young people have been influenced by educational systems to oppose free-market economics, to whitewash the human toll of Marxism, and to turn to socialism and other forms of extremist ideology.[249]

Thus, governments have an obligation to offer universal school-choice programs that empower all parents to decide the best educational setting for their children. States like Nevada and Arizona have recently enacted universal education-savings-account programs, where parents can access individual government-funded accounts to pay for education expenses for their children, including private school tuition.

And parents are strongly voicing their support for school-choice options. In 2017 in deep blue California, the respected Public Policy Institute of California found that two-thirds of public-school parents, 66 percent, supported government-funded vouchers to help parents pay for private-school tuition for their children.[250] It is no coincidence that many of the examples in this book come from California. Empirical research is a very important supplement to the case for school choice. Remember, however, that the Berlin Wall fell because people responded to the moral appeal of freedom, not because of Pentagon figures on missile throw weights.[251]

Thus, it is the obvious corruption in America's classrooms that is the most convincing argument for freedom of choice in education.

Endnotes

Endnotes

1   "The latest ranking of countries in math, reading, and science is out – and the U.S. didn't crack the top 10," *The Business Insider,* December 6, 2016, available at http://www. businessinsider. com/pisa-worldwide-ranking-of-math-science-reading-skills-2016-12

2   "Student Scores in Reading and Math Drop," *U.S. News and World Report,* October 28, 2015, available at http://www. usnews. com/news/articles/2015/10/28/student-scores-in-reading-and-math-drop

3   "What they are, why they matter and how your school scored," *Los Angeles Times,* August 24, 2016, available at http://www. latimes. com/projects/la-me-edu-test-scores-2016/

4   Greg Forster, "A Win-Win Solution: The Empirical Evidence for School Choice," *EdChoice,* May 2016, p. 1, available at http://www. edchoice. org/wp-content/uploads/2016/05/2016-5-Win-Win-Solution-WEB. pdf

5   Ibid.

6   Jonathan Mills, Anna Egalite and Patrick Wolf, "How Has the Louisiana Scholarship Program Affected Students," Education Research Alliance for New Orleans, February 22, 2016, p. 1, available at http://educationresearchalliancenola.org/files/publications/ERA-Policy-Brief-Public-Private-School-Choice-160218. pdf

7   "Teachers union: Trump's comments encourage school bullies," *The Hill*, May 5, 2015, available at http://origin-nyi.thehill.com/regulation/278911-teachers-union-trumps-comments-encourage-school-bullies

8   "National Education Association Launches Campaign to Highlight the 'Trump Effect" as Bullying Increases in Classrooms," National Education Association, October 3, 2016, available at http://www.nea.org/home/68560. htm

9   Maureen, Costello, "The Trump Effect," Southern Poverty Law Center, 2016, p. 4, available at https://www.splcenter.org/sites/default/files/splc_the_trump_effect. pdf

10   Fakhra Shah, "Anti-Hate Lesson Plan," United Educators of San Francisco, available at https://docs.google.com/document/d/15EufIKKQvIaNMDTh2aoOD2QdeKI9JXSy0MfEfh2aKnA/edit?ts=582e4597

11   Fakhra Shah, "Anti-Hate Lesson Plan," United Educators of San Francisco, available at https://docs.google.com/document/d/15EufIKKQvIaNMDTh2aoOD2QdeKI9JXSy0MfEfh2aKnA/edit?ts=582e4597

12   Ibid.

13   Ibid.

14 Ibid.

15 "FBI investigates threat against Berkeley school after teacher's counterprotest at neo-Nazi rally," *The San Jose Mercury News*, June 28, 2016, available at http://www. mercurynews.com/2016/06/28/fbi-investigates-threat-against-berkeley-school-after-teachers-counterprotest-at-neo-nazi-rally/

16 "Free Speech Rally in Berkeley results in several injuries, 20 arrests." *The Daily Californian*, April 15, 2017, available at http://www.dailycal. org/2017/04/15/free-speech-rally-berkeley-results-several-injuries-least-4-arrests/

17 "Berkeley protests of Yiannopoulos caused $100,000 in damage," *CNN. com*, February 2, 2017, available at http://www.cnn.com/2017/02/01/us/milo-yiannopoulos-berkeley/

18 "FBI investigates threat against Berkeley school after teacher's counterprotest at neo-Nazi rally," The San Jose Mercury News, June 28, 2016, available at http://www.mercurynews.com/2016/06/28/fbi-investigates-threat-against-berkeley-school-after-teachers-counterprotest-at-neo-nazi-rally/

19 Ibid.

20 "Students Hit President Trump's Face On Piñata, Teacher Suspended," *CBS Denver*, May 7, 2017, available at http://denver.cbslocal.com/2017/05/07/johnstown-pinata-trump-colorado/

21 "Staten Island teacher in Trump assignment is disciplined," *Staten Island Advance*, February 17, 2017, available at http://www.silive.com/news/index. ssf/2017/02/staten_island_teacher_in_trump. html

22 Ibid.

23   Ibid.

24   "Mountain View teacher suspended for comparing Trump to Hitler," *San Francisco Chronicle,* November 13, 2016, available at http://www.sfgate.com/bayarea/article/Mountain-View-teacher-suspended-for-comparing-10610974. php

25   "North Carolina teacher's alleged Trump comments stir controversy," *Charlotte News Observer,* September 27, 2016, available at http://www. charlotteobserver. com/news/politics-government/article104403211. html

26   "North Carolina high school teacher made her students compare speeches by Hitler and Trump, say outraged parents," *Daily Mail,* September 23, 2016, available at http://www.dailymail.co.uk/news/article-3804928/North-Carolina-high-school-teacher-students-compare-speeches-Hitler-Trump-say-outraged-parents. html#ixzz4OrIOUDr5

27   Todd Starnes, "Heil Donald? Students instructed to compare Hitler to Trump," *FoxNews. com,* September 23, 2016, available at http://www.foxnews.com/opinion/2016/09/23/heil-donald-students-instructed-to-compare-hitler-to-trump. html

28   "Dallas ISD suspends Adamson teacher over faux-assassination of Trump with water gun," *Dallas Morning News,* January 26, 2017, available at http://www. dallasnews. com/news/dallas-isd/2017/01/26/dallas-isd-teacher-hot-water-overfaux-assassination-trump-water-gun

29   "Portsmouth teacher dances to 'F--- Donald Trump," *Seacoastonline. com,* November 1, 2016, available at http://www.seacoastonline.com/news/20161031/portsmouth-teacher-dances-to-f----donald-trump

30 "Black student says teacher punched him, offered students extra credit for going to anti-Trump rally," *TheBlaze. com,* February 1, 2017, available at http://www.theblaze.com/news/2017/02/01/black-student-says-teacher-punched-him-offered-students-extra-credit-for-going-to-anti-trump-rally/

31 "To be white is to be racist," Norman student offended by teacher's lecture," kfor.com, October 18, 2016, available at http://kfor.com/2016/10/14/to-be-white-is-to-be-racist-norman-student-offended-by-teachers-lecture/

32 Ibid.

33 Ibid.

34 Todd Starnes, "Did School Promote Communism over Capitalism," radio.foxnews.com, available at http://radio.foxnews.com/toddstarnes/top-stories/did-school-promote-communism-over-capitalism.html

35 Ibid.

36 Gerald Molen, "Hollywood Producer Too Conservative for Montana High School," *Daily Inter Lake,* May 26, 2012, available at http://www.dailyinterlake.com/archive/article-1c1edc80-a747-11e1-85a7-0019bb2963f4. html

37 Ibid.

38 Ibid.

39 "United States History and Geography: Continuity and Change in Modern United States History," California State Board of Education, July 14, 2016, pp. 551, available at http://www.cde.ca. gov/ci/hs/cf/sbedrafthssfw. asp

40   Stephane Courtois, et al, *The Black Book of Communism* (Cambridge, MA and London, England: Harvard University Press, 1999), p. 4.

41   "Grade Ten – World History, Culture and Geography: The Modern World," California State Board of Education, July 14, 2016, pp. 482-83, available at http://www. cde. ca. gov/ci/hs/cf/sbedrafthssfw. asp

42   Stephane Courtois, et al, *The Black Book of Communism* (Cambridge, MA and London, England: Harvard University Press, 1999), p. 495.

43   Ibid, p. 493.

44   Ibid, pp. 493-4.

45   Ibid, p. 492.

46   Ibid, p. 513.

47   Ibid. , p. 4.

48   Ibid. , p. x.

49   "United States History and Geography: Continuity and Change in Modern United States History," California State Board of Education, July 14, 2016, p. 571, available at http://www.cde.ca.gov/ci/hs/cf/sbedrafthssfw. asp

50   Stephane Courtois, et al, *The Black Book of Communism* (Cambridge, MA and London, England: Harvard University Press, 1999), p. 572.

51   Ibid.

52   Ibid. , p. 4.

53   Jane Mansbridge, *Why We Lost the ERA* (University of Chicago Press, 1986), p. 10.

54   Judith Glazer-Raymo, *Shattering the Myths: Women in Academe* (John Hopkins University Press, 2001), p. 19.

55 "The presidential race enters the classroom," *The Economist,* October 21, 2016, available at http://www. economist. com/blogs/democracyinamerica/2016/10/ teaching-trump

56 "Shoals mother says daughter's injuries are a result of bullying, claims school isn't doing enough about it," WHNT-TV, February 6, 2017, available at http://whnt.com/2017/02/06/shoals-mother-says-daughters-injuries-a-result-of-bullying-claims-school-isnt-doing-enough-about-it/

57 "I just want them safe at school: Girl inured in Alabama 'bullying' incident," *AL. com,* February 7, 2017, available at http://www.al.com/news/huntsville/ index.ssf/2017/02/i_just_want_them_safe_at_schoo. html

58 Ibid.

59 Ibid.

60 Ibid.

61 Anlan Zhang, Lauren Musu-Gillette, and Barbara Oudekerk, "Indicators of School Crime and Safety: 2015," U.S. Department of Education and the U.S. Department of Justice Office of Justice Programs, May 2016, p.2, available at https://www.bjs.gov/ content/pub/pdf/iscs15.pdf

62 Ibid, p. 44.

63 Ibid, p. v.

64 Ibid. , p. 42.

65 Ibid.

66 Ibid, pp. vi-vii.

67 Ibid. , p. 44.

68 Ibid.

69 Katherine Kersten, "No Thug Left Behind," *City Journal*, Winter 2017, available at https://www. city-journal. org/html/no-thug-left-behind-14951. html

70 Ibid.

71 Ibid.

72 Ibid.

73 Ibid.

74 Ibid.

75 Ibid.

76 Ibid.

77 Ibid.

78 "Distrust and Disorder: A Racial Equity Policy Summons Chaos in the St. Paul Schools," *City Pages*, May 27, 2015, available at http://www. citypages. com/news/distrust-and-disorder-a-racial-equity-policy-summons-chaos-in-the-st-paul-schools-7394479

79 Anlan Zhang, Lauren Musu-Gillette, and Barbara Oudekerk, "Indicators of School Crime and Safety: 2015," U.S. Department of Education and the U.S. Department of Justice Office of Justice Programs, May 2016, p. v, available at https://www.bjs.gov/content/pub/pdf/iscs15.pdf

80 Ibid, p. iii.

81 Ibid, p. iv.

82 Ibid, p. 92.

83 Ibid, p. viii.

84 Ibid, pp. vi-vii.

85 Ibid, p. vi.

86 Of the 6.6 million suspensions, 3.4 million were in-school suspensions, while 3.2 million were out-of-school suspensions. As a percentage of the total public school population, 7 percent received in-school suspensions and 6 percent received out-of-school suspensions. See Anlan Zhang, Lauren Musu-Gillette, and Barbara Oudekerk, "Indicators of School Crime and Safety: 2015," U.S. Department of Education and the U.S. Department of Justice Office of Justice Programs, May 2016, p. 98, available at https://www. bjs. gov/content/pub/pdf/iscs15. pdf

87 Max Eden, "School Discipline Reform and Disorder: Evidence from New York City Public Schools, 2012-16," Manhattan Institute, March 2017, p. 5, available at https://www.manhattan-institute.org/sites/default/files/R-ME-0217. pdf

88 Ibid, pp. 7-8.

89 Ibid, p. 9.

90 Ibid, p. 8.

91 Ibid.

92 "Joint 'Dear Colleague Letter,'" U.S. Department of Justice Civil Rights Division and U.S. Department of Education Office of Civil Rights, January 8, 2014, available at https://www2.ed.gov/about/offices/list/ocr/letters/colleague-201401-title-vi. html

93 Ibid.

94 Max Eden, "School Discipline Reform and Disorder: Evidence from New York City Public Schools, 2012-16," Manhattan Institute, March 2017, p. 8, available at https://www.manhattan-institute.org/sites/default/files/R-ME-0217. pdf

95 John Paul Wright, et al, "Prior problem behavior accounts for the racial gap in school suspensions," *Journal of Criminal Justice,* 2014, available at https://c8.nrostatic.com/sites/default/files/pdf_article_040214_KC_HeatherMac. pdf

96 Ibid.

97 Ibid.

98 Ibid.

99 Ibid.

100 Max Eden, "School Discipline Reform and Disorder: Evidence from New York City Public Schools, 2012-16," Manhattan Institute, March 2017, p. 9, available at https://www.manhattan-institute.org/sites/default/files/R-ME-0217. pdf

101 Scott Carrell and Mark Hoekstra, "Domino Effect," EducationNext, Summer 2009, Vol. 9, No. 3, available at http://educationnext. org/domino-effect-2/

102 Ibid.

103 Ibid.

104 Ibid.

105 Max Eden, "School Discipline Reform and Disorder: Evidence from New York City Public Schools, 2012-16," Manhattan Institute, March 2017, p. 11, available at https://www.manhattan-institute.org/sites/default/files/R-ME-0217. pdf

106 Ibid.

107 Ibid, p. 9.

108 Max Eden, "School Discipline Reform and Disorder: Evidence from New York City Public Schools, 2012-16," Manhattan Institute, March 2017, p. 17\1,

available at https://www.manhattan-institute.org/sites/default/files/R-ME-0217. pdf

109 Lauren Sartain, et al, "Suspending Chicago's Students," University of Chicago Consortium on Chicago School Research, September 2015, p. 3, available at https://consortium. uchicago. edu/sites/default/files/publications/Suspending%20Chicagos%20Students. pdf

110 "Black teacher slams 'white privilege' training: 'They are hurting black kids,'" EAGnews ,May 27, 2015, available at http://eagnews. org/black-teacher-slams-white-privilege-training-they-are-hurting-black-kids/

111 Ibid.

112 Katherine Kersten, "No Thug Left Behind," *City Journal,* Winter 2017, available at https://www. city-journal. org/html/no-thug-left-behind-14951. html

113 "Facing the race issue: St. Paul schools use California-based group in effort to reduce achievement gap," *Pioneer Press,* October 27, 2013, available at http://www.twincities.com/2013/10/27/facing-the-race-issue-st-paul-schools-use-california-based-group-in-effort-to-reduce-achievement-gap/

114 Ibid.

115 Ibid.

116 Ibid.

117 Ibid.

118 Ibid.

119 "Black teacher slams 'white privilege' training: 'They are hurting black kids,'" EAGnews, May 27, 2015, available at http://eagnews. org/black-teacher-slams-

white-privilege-training-they-are-hurting-black-kids/

120 Ibid.

121 Katherine Kersten, "No Thug Left Behind," *City Journal,* Winter 2017, available at https://www. city-journal. org/html/no-thug-left-behind-14951. html

122 "Distrust and Disorder: A Racial Equity Policy Summons Chaos in the St. Paul Schools," *City Pages,* may 27, 2015, available at http://www. citypages. com/news/distrust-and-disorder-a-racial-equity-policy-summons-chaos-in-the-st-paul-schools-7394479

123 Ibid.

124 Ibid.

125 Ibid.

126 Katherine Kersten, "No Thug Left Behind," *City Journal,* Winter 2017, available at https://www. city-journal.org/html/no-thug-left-behind-14951.html

127 Max Eden, "School Discipline Reform and Disorder: Evidence from New York City Public Schools, 2012-16," Manhattan Institute, March 2017, p. 17, available at https://www.manhattan-institute.org/sites/default/files/R-ME-0217.pdf

128 Ibid, p. 18.

129 Ibid, pp. 21-22.

130 Ibid, p. 24. Max Eden, "School Discipline Reform and Disorder: Evidence from New York City Public Schools, 2012-16," Manhattan Institute, March 2017, p. 24, available at https://www. manhattan-institute. org/sites/default/files/R-ME-0217.pdf

131 Ibid.

132 Ibid, p. 25.

133 "Pennsylvania high school gives nearly 500 students suspension notices," FoxNews. com, March 31, 2017, available at http://www. foxnews. com/us/2017/03/31/pennsylvania-high-school-gives-nearly-500-students-suspension-notices.html

134 Ibid.

135 Ibid.

136 Heather Mac Donald, "Undisciplined: The Obama Administration Undermines Classroom Order in Pursuit of Phantom Racism," *City Journal*, Sumer 2012, available at https://www.city-journal.org/html/undisciplined-13485.html

137 Terry Abbott, "More teachers are having sex with their students. Here's how schools can stop them.," *Washington Post*, January 2015, available at https://www.washingtonpost.com/posteverything/wp/2015/01/20/more-teachers-are-having-sex-with-their-students-heres-how-schools-can-stop-them/?utm_term=. ef8089adfd4e

138 Ibid.

139 Ibid.

140 Ibid.

141 Ibid.

142 Ibid.

143 "Teacher Dismissal Bill (AB 215) Signed Into Law – Is It Enough?," Schools Legal Services, July 8, 2014, available at http://schoolslegalservice.org/wp-content/uploads/sites/15/2010/06/Teacher-Dismissal-Bill-AB-215-Signed-Is-it-Enough-KAL.pdf

144 Ibid.

145 Ibid.

146 "Just In: Teacher jail numbers rise to 181, costing L. A. Unified $15 million," *LA School Report*, June 22, 2016, available at http://laschoolreport. com/just-in-teacher-jail-numbers-rise-to-181-costing-la-unified-15-million/

147 Ibid.

148 Ibid.

149 Ibid.

150 "City pays exiled teachers to snooze, while 'rubber rooms' return," *New York Post*, January 17, 2016, available at http://nypost. com/2016/01/17/city-pays-exiled-teachers-to-snooze-as-rubber-rooms-return/

151 Ibid.

152 Ibid.

153 Distrust and Disorder: A Racial Equity Policy Summons Chaos in the St. Paul Schools," *City Pages*, may 27, 2015, available at http://www.citypages.com/news/distrust-and-disorder-a-racial-equity-policy-summons-chaos-in-the-st-paul-schools-7394479

154 Katherine Kersten, "No Thug Left Behind," *City Journal*, Winter 2017, available at https://www.city-journal.org/html/no-thug-left-behind-14951. html

155 Vicki Alger and Evelyn Stacey, "Safety Opportunity Scholarships (SOS): How States Can Fulfill the Promise of Safe Schools for All Students," Independent Women's Forum, 2012, p. 24. The report contains model state legislation on Safety Opportunity Scholarships. The report is available at http://www. iwf. org/files/1b668cdab62cadb07456c3497921ceda. pdf

156 "Why families choose school vouchers," *Indianapolis Star,* March 23, 2017, available at http://www. indystar.com/story/news/education/2017/03/23/ why-families-choose-school-vouchers/96837618/

157 Ibid.

158 Ibid.

159 "Looming deficits could push L. A. Unified into bankruptcy, panel says," *Los Angeles Times,* November 5, 2017, available at http://www.latimes.com/local/ lanow/la-me-ln-future-lausd-deficit-20151104-story. html

160 Ibid.

161 Ibid.

162 Ibid.

163 Ibid.

164 "L. A. Unified finds money to expand health benefits despite budget worries," *Los Angeles Times,* August 24, 2016, available at http://www.latimes.com/local/ lanow/la-me-edu-lausd-expands-health-benefits-20160823-snap-story. html

165 Susan Shelley, ""Cadillac benefits for school workers will force cuts in classroom," *Los Angeles Daily News,* September 6, 2016, available at http://www. dailynews.com/social-affairs/20160906/cadillac-benefits-for-school-workers-will-force-cuts-in-the-classroom-susan-shelley

166 "L. A. Unified finds money to expand health benefits despite budget worries," *Los Angeles Times,* August 24, 2017, available at http://www. latimes.com/local/ lanow/la-me-edu-lausd-expands-health-benefits-20160823-snap-story.html

167 Ibid.

168 Ibid.

169 "Looming deficits could push L. A. Unified into bankruptcy, panel says," *Los Angeles Times,* November 5, 2017, available at http://www. latimes.com/local/lanow/la-me-ln-future-lausd-deficit-20151104-story.html

170 Susan Shelley, ""Cadillac benefits for school workers will force cuts in classroom," *Los Angeles Daily News,* September 6, 2016, available at http://www.dailynews.com/social-affairs/20160906/cadillac-benefits-for-school-workers-will-force-cuts-in-the-classroom-susan-shelley

171 Ibid.

172 "LAUSD notifies county and state of $1. 46 billion deficit," *LA School Report,* December 15, 2016, available at http://laschoolreport.com/lausd-notifies-county-and-state-of-1-46-billion-deficit/

173 Ibid.

174 Ibid.

175 Josh McGee, "Chicago Crowd-Out," Manhattan Institute, May 2016, p. 5, available at https://www.manhattan-institute.org/sites/default/files/IB-JM-0516. pdf

176 Ibid, p. 9.

177 Ibid, p. 10.

178 Ibid, p. 9.

179 Michael Lucci, "Illinois Needs to End the Third-Party Payer Problem for Teacher Pensions," March 24, 2017, available at https://www. illinoispolicy. org/illinois-needs-to-end-the-third-party-payer-problem-for-teacher-pensions/

180 Ibid.

181 Ibid.

182 Ibid.

183 Ibid.

184 "Baltimore City schools CEO looks to deep staff cuts to lose $130 million budget gap," *The Baltimore Sun,* January 27, 2017, available at http://www.baltimoresun.com/news/maryland/education/k-12/bs-md-ci-school-budget-cuts-20170126-story. html

185 Ibid.

186 Ibid.

187 "Baltimore schools face $129 million budget deficit," *The Baltimore Sun,* December, 14, 2016, available at http://www.baltimoresun.com/news/maryland/education/bs-md-ci-city-school-deficit-20161214-story. html

188 "Raises Will Follow Raises at Cash-Strapped San Diego Unified," *Voice of San Diego,* December 12, 2016, available at http://www.voiceofsandiego.org/topics/education/layoffs-will-follow-raises-cash-strapped-san-diego-unified/

189 "Can San Diego Unified afford teacher raises?," *San Diego Union Tribune,* November 11, 2016, available at http://www.sandiegouniontribune.com/sd-me-teacher-raises-20161110-story. html

190 "Raises Will Follow Raises at Cash-Strapped San Diego Unified," *Voice of San Diego,* December 12, 2016, available at http://www.voiceofsandiego.org/topics/education/layoffs-will-follow-raises-cash-strapped-san-diego-unified/

191 Ibid.

192 "Can San Diego Unified afford teacher raises?," *San Diego Union Tribune,* November 11, 2016, available at http://www.sandiegouniontribune.com/sd-me-teacher-raises-20161110-story. html

193 "PED takes over finances at Espanola School District," kob. com, November 18, 2016, available at http://www.kob.com/new-mexico-news/public-education-department-finances-espanola-school-district-controversy-scandal-ridden-new-mexico-state/4321374/

194 Ibid.

195 "Are state takeovers fixing Mississippi's failing districts?," *Hechinger Report,* March 26, 2014, available at http://hechingerreport.org/state-takeovers-fixing-mississippis-failing-districts/

196 "Governing Urban Schools in the Future: What's Facing Philadelphia and Pennsylvania," Pew Charitable Trust, January 2016, p. 7, available at http://www.pewtrusts.org/en/research-and-analysis/issue-briefs/2016/01/governing-urban-schools-in-the-future-whats-facing-philadelphia-and-pennsylvania

197 Todd Starnes, "School orders boy to 'tolerate' undressing with girl and make it 'natural,'" FoxNews. com, March 22, 2017, available at http://www.foxnews.com/opinion/2017/03/22/school-orders-boy-to-tolerate-undressing-with-girl-and-make-it-natural. html

198 "Conservative groups sue Berks school district over transgender student," *The Philadelphia Inquirer,* March 21, 2017, available at http://www.philly.com/philly/education/Religious-groups-sue-school-district-over-transgender-student. html

199 Ibid.

200 Ibid.

201 "School Orders a Boy to Undress Next to a Girl," Snopes. com, March 26, 2017, available at http://www.snopes.com/2017/03/26/school-orders-boy-undress-next-girl/

202 "Conservative groups sue Berks school district over transgender student," *The Philadelphia Inquirer,* March 21, 2017, available at http://www.philly.com/philly/education/Religious-groups-sue-school-district-over-transgender-student. html

203 "Health textbook too explicit for some East Bay parents," *San Francisco Chronicle,* August 24, 2014, available at http://www.sfgate.com/education/article/Health-textbook-too-explicit-for-some-East-Bay-5670660. php

204 Michael Teague, Sara Mackenzie and David Rosenthal, *Your Health Today* (McGraw Hill Higher Education, 2012), p. 249.

205 Ibid.

206 Ibid.

207 Ibid, p. 259.

208 "Health textbook too explicit for some East Bay parents," *San Francisco Chronicle,* August 24, 2014, available at http://www.sfgate.com/education/article/Health-textbook-too-explicit-for-some-East-Bay-5670660. php

209 Ibid.

210 Ibid.

211 Ibid.

212 Ibid.

213 "Parents alarmed by frank sex education in school textbook," *New York Daily News,* August 8, 2014, available at http://www.nydailynews.com/life-style/parents-alarmed-frank-sex-education-california-high-school-textbook-article-1. 1896713

214 "Controversial sex-ed textbook sparks petition from California parents," today.com, August 7, 2014, available at http://www.today.com/parents/sex-ed-textbook-your-health-today-sparks-petition-parents-fremont-1D80035523

215 "Cupertino Schools: New sex-ed curriculum fails to pass after parent uproar," *San Jose Mercury News,* March 29, 2017, available at http://www.mercurynews.com/2017/03/29/cupertino-schools-new-sex-ed-curriculum-fails-to-pass-after-parent-uproar/

216 Ibid.

217 Ibid.

218 Ibid.

219 "Parents Protest Graphic Sex Ed Curriculum Changes In Cupertino Schools," 5KPIX, March 29, 2017, available at http://sanfrancisco. cbslocal.com/2017/03/29/parents-protest-graphic-sex-ed-curriculum-changes-in-cupertino-schools/

220 Ibid.

221 Ibid.

222 "Cupertino Schools: New sex-ed curriculum fails to pass after parent uproar," *San Jose Mercury News,* March 29, 2017, available at http://www.mercurynews.com/2017/03/29/cupertino-schools-new-sex-ed-curriculum-fails-to-pass-after-parent-uproar/

223 "Chatham Middle School Students Are Taught that Islam is the True Faith; Two Mothers Pilloried for Making It Public," Thomas More Law Center, March 30, 2017, available at https://www. thomasmore. org/press-releases/chatham-middle-school-students-taught-islam-true-faith-two-mothers-pilloried-making-public-must-see-video/

224 "New Jersey School District Teaches Islam But Censors Christianity," *Daily Wire*, February 21, 2017, available at http://www.dailywire.com/news/13698/new-jersey-school-district-teaches-islam-censors-aaron-bandler

225 "Chatham Middle School Students Are Taught that Islam is the True Faith; Two Mothers Pilloried for Making It Public," Thomas More Law Center, March 30, 2017, available at https://www.thomasmore.org/press-releases/chatham-middle-school-students-taught-islam-true-faith-two-mothers-pilloried-making-public-must-see-video/

226 "New Jersey School District Teaches Islam But Censors Christianity," *Daily Wire*, February 21, 2017, available at http://www.dailywire.com/news/13698/new-jersey-school-district-teaches-islam-censors-aaron-bandler

227 Ibid.

228 Ibid.

229 "Chatham Middle School Students Are Taught that Islam is the True Faith; Two Mothers Pilloried for Making It Public," Thomas More Law Center, March 30, 2017, available at https://www.thomasmore.org/press-releases/chatham-middle-school-students-taught-islam-true-faith-two-mothers-pilloried-making-public-must-see-video/

230 Parents question seventh-grade lesson on Islam," *newjerseyhills. com,* February 10, 2017, available at http://www.newjerseyhills.com/chatham_courier/parents-question-seventh-grade-lesson-on-islam/article_5b7d9d73-aa18-58be-8bbc-0e1b77fc969e.html

231 Melissa and John Kevin Wood v. Charles County Public Schools, et al, Case 8:16-cv-00239-GJH, Document 1, filed January 27, 2016, pp. 2-3, available at https://www.thomasmore.org/wp-content/uploads/2016/01/Thomas-More-Law-Center-Files-Lawsuit-On-Behalf-of-Marine-Dad-Banned-from-Schoo-After-He-Objected-to-Islamic-Indoctrination-Complaint-Time-Stamped. pdf

232 Ibid, p. 10.

233 Ibid, p. 11-12.

234 Ibid, p. 13.

235 Ibid, p. 16.

236 Ibid, p. 11.

237 Ibid, p. 15.

238 Ibid, p. 16.

239 Ibid, p. 3.

240 Ibid, p. 2, citing *Santa Fe Independent School District v. Doe,* U.S. 290, pp. 309-310 (2000).

241 Ibid, p. 19.

242 "San Diego schools sued over anti-Islamophobia campaign," Associated Press, May 26, 2017, available at http://abcnews.go.com/US/wireStory/san-diego-schools-sued-anti-islamophobia-campaign-47649401

243 Citizens for Quality Education, et al vs. San Diego Unified School District, et al, Complaint for Declaratory and Injunctive Relief and Nominal Damages, Case No. '17 CV 1054 BAS JMA, United States District for the Southern District of California, p 10, available at https://www.investigativeproject. org/documents/case_docs/3327.pdf

244 "Parents Sue San Diego School District Over 'Initiative to Combat Islamophobia," *Christian News,* May 29, 2017, available at http://christiannews. net/2017/05/29/parents-sue-san-diego-school-district-over-initiative-to-combat-islamophobia/

245 Inez Feltscher Stepman, "State Lawmakers Need to Dramatically Increase School Choice Now or America is Over," *The Federalist,* February 14, 2017, available at http://thefederalist.com/2017/02/14/state-lawmakers-need-dramatically-increase-school-choice-now-america/

246 https://today.yougov.com/news/2015/05/11/one-third-millennials-like-socialism/

247 Marion Smith, "100 Years of Communism's Bloody History," *The Daily Beast,* April 22, 2017, available at http://www.thedailybeast.com/articles/2017/04/23/100-years-the-birth-of-socialism.html

248 Ibid.

249 Ibid.

250 "Californians and Education," Public Policy Institute of California, April 2017, p. 3, available at http://www.ppic.org/content/pubs/survey/S_417MBS.pdf

251 Ibid.

About the Author

LANCE IZUMI

Lance Izumi is Koret Senior Fellow in Education Studies and Senior Director of the Center for Education at the Pacific Research Institute, a public policy think tank based in San Francisco, Sacramento, and Pasadena, California. He is the author of numerous books, studies and articles on education policy issues, and served as co-executive producer of an award-winning PBS-broadcast documentary on underperforming middle-class public schools and co-executive producer, writer and narrator of a *New York Times*-posted short film on school choice.

In 2016-17, Lance served on President Trump's transition Agency Action Team for education policy.

From 2004 to 2015, he served as a member of the Board of Governors of the California Community Colleges, the largest system of higher education in the nation, and served two terms as president of the Board from 2008 to 2009.

In 2015, he was elected chair of the board of directors of the Foundation for California Community Colleges, the official non-profit that supports the community college system and the state Chancellor's Office.

He also served as a commissioner on the California Postsecondary Education Commission and as a member of the United States Civil Rights Commission's California Advisory Committee.

Previously, he served as chief speechwriter and director of writing and research for California Governor George Deukmejian and as speechwriter to United States

Attorney General Edwin Meese III in President Ronald Reagan's administration.

Lance received his juris doctorate from the University of Southern California School of Law, his master of arts in political science from the University of California at Davis, and his bachelor of arts in economics and history from the University of California at Los Angeles.

Researchers

Cassidy Syftestad

Cassidy Syftestad is an American Studies major at Hillsdale College and an education policy intern at the Heritage Foundation. Following graduation in 2018 and law school, she plans to return to her home state of California to affect policy change in the education arena.

Christie Syftestad

Christie Syftestad is a 4th/5th grade teacher at a California charter school. While raising her own three children, she has taught in public, private, Montessori, Classical and Title 1 schools from early elementary through high school for ten years. As a California public-school graduate, she is convinced that American education reform, most especially school choice, is imperative.

About Pacific Research Institute

The Pacific Research Institute (PRI) champions freedom, opportunity, and personal responsibility by advancing free-market policy solutions. It provides practical solutions for the policy issues that impact the daily lives of all Americans, and demonstrates why the free market is more effective than the government at providing the important results we all seek: good schools, quality health care, a clean environment, and a robust economy.

Founded in 1979 and based in San Francisco, PRI is a non-profit, non-partisan organization supported by private contributions. Its activities include publications, public events, media commentary, community leadership, legislative testimony, and academic outreach.

ACKNOWLEDGEMENTS

The author would like to thank the Koret Foundation for its support of the fellowship for the author of this book.

The author would like to thank Cassidy Syftestad and Christie Syftestad for their research assistance. He would also like to thank Lauren Geary for providing research help. The author would also like to thank Sally Pipes, president and CEO of the Pacific Research Institute; Rowena Itchon, PRI senior vice president; Tim Anaya, PRI director of communications; Dana Beigel, art director; and the other dedicated staff of the Pacific Research Institute who made this book possible. The author of this book has worked independently and his views and conclusions do not necessarily represent those of the board, supporters, or staff of PRI.

CPSIA information can be obtained
at www.ICGtesting.com
Printed in the USA
LVOW05s1622040218
565178LV00037BA/498/P